Putting the Young in Business

Policy Challenges for Youth Entrepreneurship

LEED Notebook No. 29

ORGANISATION FOR ECONOMIC CO-OPERATION AND DEVELOPMENT

ORGANISATION FOR ECONOMIC CO-OPERATION AND DEVELOPMENT

Pursuant to Article 1 of the Convention signed in Paris on 14th December 1960, and which came into force on 30th September 1961, the Organisation for Economic Co-operation and Development (OECD) shall promote policies designed:

- to achieve the highest sustainable economic growth and employment and a rising standard of living in Member countries, while maintaining financial stability, and thus to contribute to the development of the world economy;
- to contribute to sound economic expansion in Member as well as non-member countries in the process of economic development; and
- to contribute to the expansion of world trade on a multilateral, non-discriminatory basis in accordance with international obligations.

The original Member countries of the OECD are Austria, Belgium, Canada, Denmark, France, Germany, Greece, Iceland, Ireland, Italy, Luxembourg, the Netherlands, Norway, Portugal, Spain, Sweden, Switzerland, Turkey, the United Kingdom and the United States. The following countries became Members subsequently through accession at the dates indicated hereafter: Japan (28th April 1964), Finland (28th January 1969), Australia (7th June 1971), New Zealand (29th May 1973), Mexico (18th May 1994), the Czech Republic (21st December 1995), Hungary (7th May 1996), Poland (22nd November 1996), Korea (12th December 1996) and the Slovak Republic (14th December 2000). The Commission of the European Communities takes part in the work of the OECD (Article 13 of the OECD Convention).

Publié en français sous le titre :
ENCOURAGER LES JEUNES A ENTREPRENDRE
Les défis politiques

© OECD 2001

Permission to reproduce a portion of this work for non-commercial purposes or classroom use should be obtained through the Centre français d'exploitation du droit de copie (CFC), 20, rue des Grands-Augustins, 75006 Paris, France, Tel. (33-1) 44 07 47 70, Fax (33-1) 46 34 67 19, for every country except the United States. In the United States permission should be obtained through the Copyright Clearance Center, Customer Service, (508)750-8400, 222 Rosewood Drive, Danvers, MA 01923 USA, or CCC Online: http://www.copyright.com/. All other applications for permission to reproduce or translate all or part of this book should be made to OECD Publications, 2, rue André-Pascal, 75775 Paris Cedex 16, France.

Foreword

The critical role played by entrepreneurship in driving economic development and job creation is increasingly understood. But even now, in the emerging "New Economy", its potential is often not fully recognised and supported by policymakers. In terms of social cohesion, too, entrepreneurship can play an important role, allowing some of those people otherwise marginalised from the labour market to create their own opportunities to participate in economic life. One of the concerns of the OECD LEED Programme, therefore, is to stimulate policy debate on the factors that encourage entrepreneurship, the obstacles that stand in its way and the policy measures that can be developed to support it. This Notebook represents part of this effort, covering the important topic of youth entrepreneurship. It presents some of the many youth entrepreneurship programmes that have emerged at the local level in recent years. These programmes are easing the entry of young people into the labour market in a way that is making our economies stronger and more flexible. But the book also identifies some of the barriers that remain to releasing the entrepreneurial talent of young people and points to how policy approaches might be strengthened.

This stock take of developments in youth entrepreneurship policy is based on materials prepared for an international conference held by the OECD LEED Programme in Rome in November 1999, with the support of the Italian agency for youth entrepreneurship, *Imprenditorialità Giovanile*. A number of papers were commissioned for the conference, covering the policy context in countries such as Australia, Canada, France, Italy, the United Kingdom and the United States of America and examining the nature of the youth problem in our changing economies and societies. To complement this work, the LEED secretariat also carried out background research to identify, describe and compare some of the most interesting youth entrepreneurship programmes in operation in the OECD countries.

This Notebook represents a synthesis of the resulting debates and analyses. It is written by Robert Cornell, a former Deputy Secretary-General of the OECD, who was invited to give his view of the current policy challenges for youth entrepreneurship.

Table of Contents

Preface 7

Chapter 1. **Issues and Questions** 13
    Unemployed youth: The core problem 14
    National situations differ: Some examples 14
    Contrasting policy approaches 21
    Towards a definition of self-employment 23
    The state of entrepreneurship and attitudes towards it in the OECD area 25
    Concluding remarks 39

Chapter 2. **Emerging Programme Approaches to Youth Entrepreneurship** ... 41
    Introduction 41
    Some comparative country surveys 46
    Some other "best practice" examples 77
    International youth-business networks 79

Chapter 3. **Education, Training and Youth Entrepreneurship: an Analysis** ... 81
    Introduction 81
    Two definitions 84
    Teaching teachers 86
    Teaching entrepreneurship in primary, secondary and tertiary institutions ... 87
    Training 89

Chapter 4. **Conclusions and Some Policy Suggestions** 91
    The principal conclusions 91
    Some policy suggestions 93

Notes 97
Bibliography 101

Figures

1. GDP and unemployment in Canada, 1988-1998 15
2. Canadian labour force, 1988-1998 16
3. Programme to promote youth entrepreneurship: a schematic presentation ... 42

Tables

1. A snapshot of US youth unemployment 18
2. A numerical survey of self-employment in the OECD area, 1970 and 1996 26
3. Self-employment in Italy, 1980-1996, with some international comparisons 28
4. Civil employment in Italy by professional status, 1980 and 1995 29
5. Youth and self-employment in Australia, 1995 34
6. Some survey results on workplace preferences, 1989 36
7. Job satisfaction 37
8. Italian Government financial support for programmes related to labour market policies, 1998 48

Box

1. Highlights of new measures to promote enterprise creation in France, announced by the government in April 2000 54

Preface

Paul Cullen, Chair of the OECD LEED Directing Committee

This report on behalf of my Committee, the Local Economic and Employment Development Committee, gives me the opportunity to set out the continuing role of LEED in the new OECD context.

When the Local Employment Initiatives Programme was established in 1982, the then Secretary-General, Emile Van Lennep, took the view (which was shared by the Council) that only macro-economic policies could "create" jobs, except in the non-traded sector of the economy. However, slow economic growth and high unemployment put increasing pressure on Ministers of Labour to go beyond their traditional functions of facilitating the job search process and administering unemployment benefits, and to play a role in the job creation policy. Structural policies, notably those enhancing labour market flexibility, were given increasing emphasis. Today, it is a commonplace of the OECD policy stance that employment is dependent on *both* macro-economic policies *and* structural policies, without the Van Lennep limitation to the non-traded sector. LEED still speaks for local economies and communities, but local economic development is now recognised as playing a key role in employment, the more so because of the dominant globalisation process. "Think global, act local" has become one of the truisms of the day.

I sketch out the past history because it seems to me that the OECD has not yet fully adapted to what we might call the transition to the Schumpeterian as opposed to the Keynesian economy. Even the widely-praised OECD *Jobs Study* neglected somewhat the innovation process as compared with the adjustment process in modern OECD economies. Structural policies have indeed hinged more on the "flexibility" of resources, and notably labour, as opposed to the "creativity" of human capital which is inherent in the "new economy", whatever meaning is given to that term.

© OECD 2001

The central issue, it seems to me, is what Schumpeter called "creative destruction". As competition becomes more global and trade freer, it becomes more costly to protect jobs. Success is therefore dependent on a high rate of job creation, and this, in the turbulent economies of today, is highly dependent on enterprise creation. This is the logic that is bringing entrepreneurship into the centre of debate. That is why LEED, long before the OECD Jobs Study, has given priority to the conditions under which all social groups, and not only the "whizz kids" referred to by my colleague, Carlo Borgomeo, can take part in the entrepreneurial process at the local level. For it is at this level that most entrepreneurial decisions are taken.

Because of the traditional dominance of macro-economic policies the OECD's mental set has always been top-down. A new partnership is now needed between the top-down and the bottom-up approaches, because economic culture is changing in the OECD countries as they find themselves locked into a headlong pace of change. In modern democracies at the front-edge of the world economy, change has to spring from the grass roots and many more people than in the past have to take economic initiatives and accept risk. This report, *Putting the Young in Business*, examines how youth can be helped to take part in this process.

As Chairman of the LEED Directing Committee, I welcome it at a time when the OECD is beginning to debate the significance and role of the "New Economy", as at the recent Forum 2000.

Carlo Borgomeo, Vice Chair of the LEED Directing Committee and President of *Imprenditorialità Giovanile*

I am pleased to have the opportunity, as the co-sponsor of the Rome conference on youth entrepreneurship, to make a plea for a radical change of policies towards young people in the OECD countries.

In its background report for the stage-setting of the conference in Washington on "Preparing Youth for the 21st Century", the OECD Secretariat reached the sombre conclusion that *"despite a decline in the relative numbers of youth and the proliferation of programmes aimed at young people in the past two decades, their employment and earnings position has worsened, in some countries substantially"*.

No one can doubt that the costs to society and to the economy of a continuation of this situation will be enormous in the long-term. But realistically, what can be done?

My first suggestion would be to recognise that no single policy or set of policies will do the trick. Since the oil shocks of the 1970s, the slowing down of economic growth and the shrinking of job opportunities has led understandably to a policy focus on – indeed obsession with – the transition from school to work. Education policy was increasingly influenced by the German "apprenticeship' model, in which young people make an early transition to the world of work. So-called "active' labour market policies concentrated on "work experience' and training to bridge the schoolwork gap. Economic policy hammered the need to reduce the costs of employing young people, thereby enhancing labour market flexibility. But little attention has been paid to the reality that youth's position in the economy and society has changed radically, and that one of the key questions is now "transition to what?"

The simple answer to this question is that, whereas their fathers and forefathers made the transition to a world of stable and clear – even if unequal – trades and professions, the rising generation is moving into a world of occupational quick-sands and volcanoes. In this contemporary context, the question of youth entrepreneurship, as dealt with at the Rome conference, becomes vital. If the "new" economy needs to be based on a culture of entrepreneurship, as leading politicians now assert, it is obvious that to exclude youth from that culture is asking for trouble. On the contrary, policies should be directed towards facilitating and encouraging the contemporary shift in youth culture towards "doing your own thing".

This is the opportunity that has to be seized. Youth has a natural disposition for innovation and change on which we can capitalise, as long as we are clear that successfully launching a new enterprise – however small – is a process of *innovation*. That is where young people have a comparative advantage. Of course, the new information technologies are an indispensable tool, and young people have a better grasp than their elders. But the heart of the new economy is innovation in all aspects of business, including its social purposes. We could sum it up by saying that a new culture of work is emerging, and that young entrepreneurs have the capacity to understand it and to be the pioneers.

Part of this capacity is to understand that technological and social innovation are part of the same process of modernisation. Solow's productivity paradox – the slow arrival of productivity gains despite the massive US investment in computers – is no doubt thus explained. The paradox has been resolved as enterprises have come to grips with this reality, and by the massive growth of new employment-intensive services, involving the birth of something like a million new firms per annum in America. In Italy, in a recent national competition for young entrepreneurs, out of 65 000 submissions, some 6 000 were for enterprises in the broad field of entertainment: a signal of the new economic culture that is emerging.

The danger could be that this capacity for technological and social innovation could be limited to a new youth elite, the "whizz-kids" of a new entrepreneurial culture. Our Italian experience suggests the contrary. Money, tradition and education coming from social and family background are not the keys to entrepreneurial success. As the LEED Programme has demonstrated since its inception in the OECD, a popularisation and democratisation of entrepreneurship is taking place: women, the unemployed and the disadvantaged can succeed in the entrepreneurial saga if they are supported by appropriate policies. Obviously the young, and the more so those who are disadvantaged, do not have access to start-up capital and traditional banking cannot rise to the challenge. Equally obviously, although the "University of Entrepreneurship" does not and never will exist, training is a must. But the key is that one becomes an entrepreneur not by birth but by experience, so that the young entrepreneur also needs to be "tutored" by an enterprise which possesses that experience. This has to be contracted for and therefore paid for. In all these matters – money, training and experience – public policy can play an important role.

This is why, at the beginning of this Preface, I made a plea for a radical change of policies, and a broader approach, going beyond the education, training, manpower and social policies gradually built up since World War II. Full Employment and the Welfare State were the pillars on which these policies were built, and both were hinged on our understanding of the economic cycle and its relation to human welfare. The economic cycle is changing under the impact of globalisation and technological change: some talk of the "death" of the economic cycle, some of a new technological paradigm bequeathing a long cycle of growth, others of the post-industrial society. The complexities cannot be seized by any slogan, but who can deny that we have moved into a world of "creative destruction" in which the key, central, unavoidable challenge is to create the enterprises to create the jobs whose disappearance cannot be resisted. As the pace of change accelerates, the values associated with entrepreneurship – initiative, risk-taking, and creativity – penetrate all sectors of life, including basic education for the rising generation. The paradox is that security, which is as necessary as change, can only be sustained if countries succeed in generating opportunities and helping people to gain access to them. The problem of equality – inescapable in democracy – lies in the distribution and the redistribution of opportunities, especially towards young people who have been among the "losers' in the post oil-shock decades.

I hope that the Washington and Rome conferences will open up a new chapter in OECD's long-standing interest in the role of young people in society and the economy. Through the expanding youth opportunities of the post-war decades, to the student upheavals of May 1968, and on to the hard realities of the high unemployment in the 1980s and 1990s, the Organisation has stimulated new policies. We are, I believe, at a new turning point. Both culturally and economically, the OECD societies need to tap the creativity of young people and not least the new generation of young women seeking equality of opportunity. New economic opportunities are there, but they require more risk-taking than in the past. A lot will depend on the communications revolution and whether the computer and the Internet will isolate or give vent to contemporary youth's desire to relate to and express solidarity with a much wider world.

We cannot be sure of the outcome, but as policy-makers, we have to take the risk of investing lucidly in youth's capacity to find the solutions.

© OECD 2001

Chapter 1
Issues and Questions

While the creation of an enterprise is a personal and individual adventure, it is also the business of society as a whole, because its benefits are collective. Enterprise creation is indeed the key to growth and employment. In the medium term, our economy's prosperity and its standing on the world scene depend on it.

Mr. Jacques Chirac, President of France[1]

Not everyone, including many experts and bureaucrats, would agree fully with this strong policy statement, much less adapt the industrial countries' traditional unemployment, education and social safety-net policies to reflect it. The still-widespread, standard policy view of enterprise creation sees it as a matter for venture capitalists and seasoned risk takers – dynamic, perhaps, even important, but not for ordinary folk, certainly not for mere youth, and hardly relevant for public measures to deal with unemployment, including rising permanent unemployment among the young.

A growing movement challenges this orthodox view. It remains largely the domain of private groups and a few successful government programmes, notably pioneer initiatives of the Italian government. It works from three premises. First, younger people can indeed found new businesses and succeed. Second, this activity can contribute handsomely to economic dynamism and growth. Third, and for these reasons, the encouragement of youth entrepreneurship should have a place in national, regional and local labour market and education policies. Interest centres on these two policy areas for two reasons. Rising youth unemployment, often even during cyclical upswings, has proven intractable under the traditional labour-policy approaches of the industrial countries. If young entrepreneurs are to be encouraged, those traditional policies will require

© OECD 2001

adaptation. Moreover, an important element in making them effective will reside in the degree to which the educational system can inculcate the skills, attitudes and habits of mind which promise success for those who choose to go into business for themselves.

In November 1999, the Local Economic and Employment Development unit (LEED) of the OECD's Territorial Development Service, with the co-sponsorship of the Italian Agency for Youth Entrepreneurship, held a high-level conference on the subject in Rome. The conference examined developments in the field and reviewed programmes to promote youth entrepreneurship in a number of OECD countries, searching for an inventory of "best practices" in this relatively new policy area. This book reports the results of that conference. It takes the form of an extended review essay on the subject, rather than the usual "conference compendium" approach. In this form, it can serve as a basic reference document for those interested in the field.

Unemployed youth: The core problem[2]

In the industrial countries, youth unemployment tends to hover around roughly twice the adult rate. In 1999, for example, the unemployment rate for people 15-24 years of age in the European countries of the OECD area was 12 per cent, compared to 6 per cent among all adults (OECD, 2000). Countries with the most severe unemployment problems may well have a third of their young people searching for work. For the OECD area as a whole, overall unemployment remained above 6 per cent throughout the 1990s. With youth unemployment about twice as high, on average, it becomes clear that persistently large groups of young people remain stranded outside both education systems and society's workplaces, untouched and not helped by traditional economic, labour and education policies. This situation wastes human resources that could contribute to economic progress in the short run, produces widespread unhappiness and social discontent among the young, and may leave long-term scars on the working adults of the next generation.

National situations differ: Some examples

A broad-brush international survey hides many details of youth unemployment and its causes in individual countries. Papers presented at the Rome conference or as background for it, although they did not cover all the OECD Member countries in the same detail, illuminated both national differences and common problems (Grant and Dupuy, 1999; Dabson and Willson, 1999; White, 1999; Serieyx, 1998).

In *Canada*, the labour force grew steadily, by about 13 per cent in the 1988-98 decade, in line with growth of the population as a whole. The number of young people in it, however, defined as those 15-24 years old, fell by 14 per cent; it has recently begun to stabilise. Within this group, the 15-19 age cohort expanded slightly between 1994 and 1998 (by 1.4%), while the 20-24 cohort continued to shrink.[3]

As one would expect, both overall and youth unemployment followed cyclically sensitive paths, rising sharply during Canada's severest recession since the 1930s in 1990-1992, then stabilising and falling through the rest of the decade (see Figures 1 and 2). Canada's young people felt the worst effects. More cycle-sensitive in recession and less so in recovery, youth unemployment rose faster than the overall rate in the downturn, then dropped much more sluggishly as the economy rebounded (Figure 2). The numbers tell the story. Total unemployment rose 50 per cent

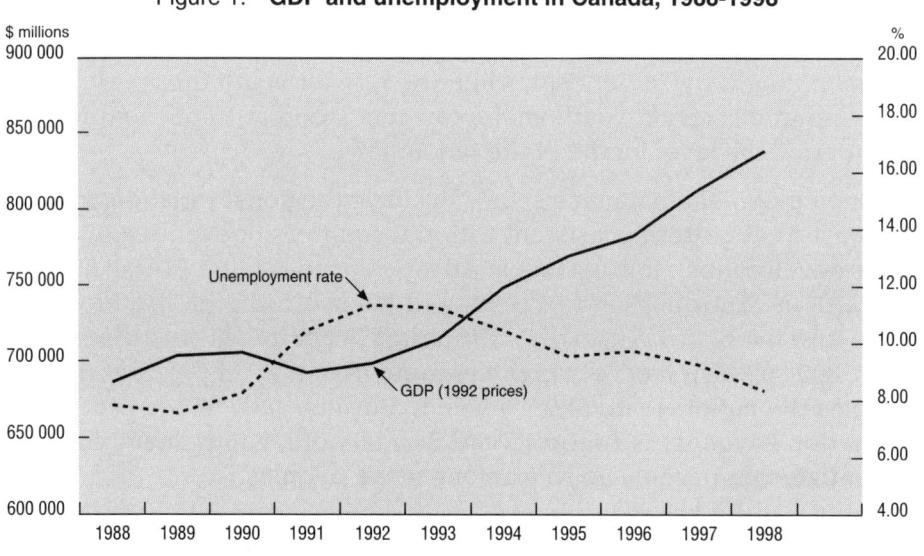

Figure 1. **GDP and unemployment in Canada, 1988-1998**

Source: Statistics Canada Catalogue 71-001, various years.

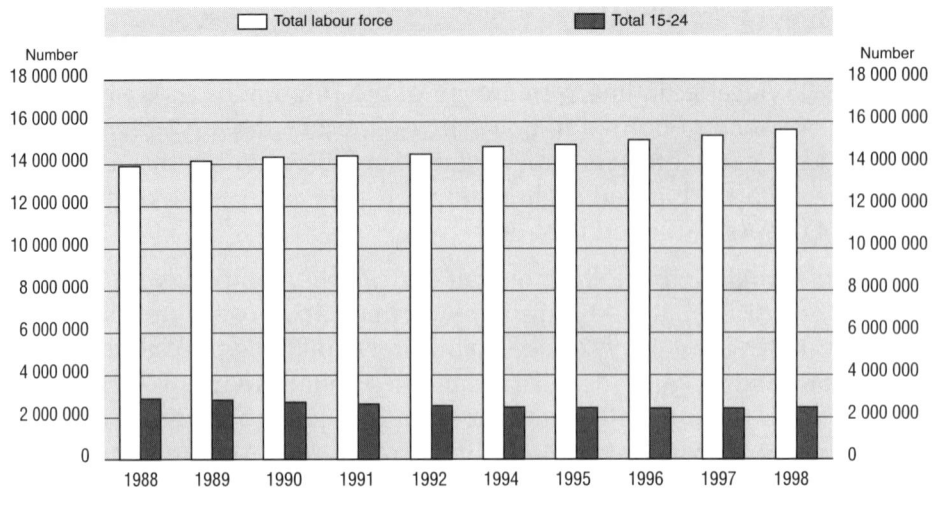

Figure 2. **Canadian labour force, 1988-1998**

Source: OECD.

between 1989 and 1992, but youth unemployment jumped by 60 per cent, from 11.2 per cent to 17.8 per cent. Thereafter, however, unemployment in general plunged by 26 per cent, while the rate for youth dropped by only 15 per cent. As a result, youth unemployment stood at 15 per cent in 1998, almost twice the level for the entire labour force.

Unemployment in Canada shows significant regional variation, in a distinct east-west pattern consistent with the country's uneven regional economic development. It is highest in Atlantic Canada (17.8% overall and 28% for youth in Newfoundland in 1998) and lowest in the Prairie Provinces (5.7% and 10.6% in Alberta).[4] Canada's Aboriginal population of nearly 800 000 also has very high unemployment, at 24 per cent in 1996, 2.5 times the national rate of 9.7 per cent. Because fully 55 per cent of this population is young, between 15 and 24 years old, youth unemployment concentrates particularly heavily among these peoples.[5]

Why do Canadian young people participate less in the active labour force than previously, and why do job prospects for the smaller proportion that remains fail to keep pace with overall employment and the expansion of the economy? The Canada paper (Grant and Dupuy, 1999) attributes high youth unemployment to changes in the Canadian workplace. Labour markets have developed more flexible work arrangements since the recovery began, including more part-time and contract work. The paper cites research that shows youth as particularly vulnerable to the "last-hired, first-fired" rule when these shifts occur. Young people have neither seniority nor significant work experience. Thus they are the first to go when an economic downturn occurs and the last to get hired, if ever, as the economy rebounds, because they compete for jobs with a big pool of previously employed, experienced older workers.

More and more young Canadians, choosing to postpone their transition from school to full-time employment in a discouraging labour market, stay in school longer and seek some work experience in the increasingly abundant part-time jobs. The paper cites information from Statistics Canada (1998) that the transition from studying without working to working without studying is lengthening and growing more complex. In 1988, it lasted about six years, from ages 15 to 21. By 1998 it had extended to eight years, from ages 16 to 24, with no guarantee of full-time work even then. Part-time work is the more likely outcome for those who eventually leave school. In 1996, some 20 per cent of all non-student jobs were part-time, a proportion triple that of two decades before, and non-student youth had a higher incidence of part-time employment than did the older part of the labour force.

In the *United States*, youth employment prospects are a function of education, race, age and gender. Education plays the largest role, regardless of the other three, as the key determinant of a person's likelihood of employment (see Table 1). Young, black males who have recently dropped out of high school face the worst of plights.

In contrast with Canada, youth labour-force participation rates more or less mirror those of the overall population and have not changed much in recent years; the data show only a hint of a decline in youths' share. Between 1994 and 1998 the youth participation rate slipped to 65.8 per cent from 66.4 per cent, while the overall rate inched upward to 67.1 per cent from 66.6 per cent. Much more important, because most 16-24 year-olds remain in school, their employment patterns show strong seasonal variation, rising in the summer and falling back when the school year resumes.

© OECD 2001

Table 1. **A snapshot of US youth unemployment**
(In per cent, latest year available, ages 16-24 years)

Overall rates, 1998		Rates by gender and age, 1997	
Total labour force, all ages	4.5	Male, 16-19	16.9
Ages 16-19	14.6	Male, 20-24	8.9
Ages 20-24 (4th quarter, 1998)	7.1	Female, 16-19	15.0
		Female, 20-24	8.1
Unemployment and educational attainment, 1998[1]		Rates by race and gender, 1995	
Doctorate	1.3	White males	15.6
Professional Degree	1.4	White females	13.4
Master's Degree	1.6	Black males	37.1
Bachelor's Degree	1.9	Black females	34.3
Associate Degree	2.5	Hispanic males	25.6
Some college, no degree	3.2	Hispanic females	22.6
High-school graduate	4.1		
Less than a high-school diploma	7.1		
Rates for recent high-school dropouts, 1997		Rates by race, ages 16-19, 1998	
Total	55.1	White	12.6
White	51.2	Black	27.6
Black	82.6	Hispanic	21.3
Hispanic (1996)	45.5		

1. Rates are for the entire labour force
Source: Dabson and Willson (1999), from US Bureau of Labor Statistics (BLS) data.

In the United States as elsewhere, youth unemployment hovers around at least twice that of the broad labour force. It is three times the overall rate for the 16-19 age cohort. Unemployment rates dropped by about a third during the sustained economic boom of the second half of the 1990s. Young men are slightly more likely than young women to face unemployment, a reversal of the situation in the overall labour force,[6] and jobless rates of all minority youth, especially black young people, remain exceptionally high.

Because educational achievement strongly overrides all other influences on what society views as employability, including age, sex and ethnic origin, people – pre-eminently youth -– with low education levels find it extremely difficult even to enter the labour force. This problem is severe. The United States has 15 million young people between the ages of 16 and 24. Some 70 per cent of them have a high school diploma or less. Young high-school dropouts fare the worst. "*Only 58 per cent of* 1995-1996 *dropouts were in the labor force, and 28 per cent of those in the labor force were unemployed. Of the 1996 high school graduates who were not in college, 78 per cent were in the labor force, and 24 per cent of those in the labor force were unemployed."* (National Center of Education Statistics, 1997, Chapter 5).

The conference paper on *Australia* (White, 1999) looks at youth unemployment somewhat less systematically, but it makes some telling points about the problem:

- Unemployment among 15-19 year olds looking for full-time work stands at three to four times that of the general population. Some 40 per cent of all unemployed Australians are under 40 years old.

- The teenage labour force (persons both unemployed and seeking work) has shrunk by 15 per cent over the last 20 years, while the overall labour force has grown by 44 per cent. Labour market demand for younger workers has declined, apparently prompting lower youth participation rates, just as in Canada (and Europe). In just the past decade the number of full-time jobs available has halved. In 1998, less than 17 per cent of young people had full-time jobs, as against 60 per cent during the 1960s (Spierings, 1998).

- More young people (15-24 years of age) now work in part-time employment than in full-time jobs. In the past two decades, the overall number of jobs in the Australian economy expanded by 40 per cent, but the part-time component of this rise, over 133 per cent, dominated that growth. White characterises this as a sustained period of "jobless growth". Youth employment concentrates in three sub-sectors: Retail Trade, Manufacturing and the services embraced by Accommodation, Cafes and Restaurants.[7]

The paper cites as explanations for these developments deep structural changes in the Australian economy, similar to those described for Canada and indeed common to all of the industrial economies in varying degrees. Fifteen per cent of Australian teenagers engage only in "marginal activity", *i.e.*, remain unemployed, work in part-time jobs while not improving their education or skills through recognised study, or have left the labour market. Labour markets for young people, highly fragmented, offer mostly casual jobs – 55 per cent now, as against 24 per cent in 1984. An estimated 10 per cent of teenagers spend their late teenage years in intermittent casual work and unemployment, falling steadily behind those remaining in education to advance their employable skills. More than

© OECD 2001

300 000 work in mostly low-skilled part-time or casual jobs while studying full time. Over 60 000 struggle to find full-time work and nearly 13 000 have had no employment for over a year (Spierings, 1998).

This structural context often includes insecure and sometimes poorly paid employment that demands flexibility and multiple skills in rapidly changing workplaces. Inexperienced young people without training rarely possess these attributes. Yet, looking ahead to the potential for self-employment and entrepreneurship among the young if they are appropriately helped, the structural context also contains both the conditions and the skill requirements for successful self-employment. White points out that the necessary adaptations of today's young people to future work situations will face them with:

- Employment patterns characterised by uncertain combinations of traditional jobs, casual and contract work, jobs in the informal economy, retraining stints and periods of outright unemployment.
- A tendency towards flat organisational structures that require employees to take more responsibility for making decisions, work in teams, deploy multiple skills and be both flexible and creative.
- More opportunities to choose self-employment and increasing use of subcontracting arrangements for tasks that firms traditionally performed in-house, with permanent employees.
- A rising tendency to operate home-based businesses.[8]

The Serieyx paper (1998) points out that in *Europe* as well, people aged 16-25 face unemployment double that of older workers (25-55).[9] Rising long-term unemployment among the young generates hopelessness (of which rising suicide rates are one symptom) and a sort of inurement that works against entry or re-entry to working life. Governments have come to see the problems as so pervasive that they are broadening the coverage of some of their programmes for the "young" in the labour force – to age 30 in France and the United Kingdom, 35 in Germany and even 38 for certain measures for southern Italy.

This paper echoes the others in highlighting the impacts of workplace changes, and changes in the nature of work itself, on European youth labour markets. The increased competition associated with globalisation pushes firms to concentrate on core activities, increasingly farming out non-core tasks to sub-contractors, which themselves must concentrate and focus on core competencies. This leads to fewer permanent jobs and more fixed-term contracts even within firms, more self-employment and more temporary work. Indeed, the fixed-term contract is now the norm for younger workers' first jobs; only seasoned professionals get indefinite-term jobs in the traditional sense. The new patterns of production management, changing from job-based to process-based organisation, from separate functions to work flows and from task-oriented to project-centred operations, place a premium on not only experience but also abilities for interactive teamwork, flexibility and creativity. Older workers with experience have difficulty adapting to the new methods. Younger ones have neither the experience nor the training, because traditional education systems fail to meet the labour markets' new needs.

The primary impact of these shifts on the youth labour force becomes precisely what the Canadian experience has shown. Economic growth no longer can solve the youth unemployment problem, because structural changes in the economy cause jobs for youth to dry up very rapidly in cyclical downturns and then not adequately materialise in the upswings. Youth unemployment thus entrenches itself in a structural impasse, which traditional labour market policies simply cannot touch.

Contrasting policy approaches

All of the industrial countries have long devoted considerable political attention and economic resources to labour market policies. Despite national differences in organisation and emphasis, they all have three main components. The first and most resource-intensive involves income support, the social safety-net policies which provide the unemployed with financial benefits intended to tide them over with family income during their time of unemployment. Eligibility for such benefits usually requires prior full-time employment and that the unemployment be involuntary. The benefits usually end after fixed periods, although the emergence of more long-term unemployment has prompted many governments to extend them. The second component seeks to correct labour market failures by helping the unemployed to find jobs. Its most common form is the labour-office approach, under which employers report job openings and unemployed workers appear at official labour offices to be matched with them. Sometimes labour unions perform this function as well. The third component involves government-run or subsidised training and "retraining" programmes. As they have struggled to deal with the labour market impacts of the structural and workplace changes described in the preceding section,

© OECD 2001

governments probably have tinkered with this element more than either of the other two, and often with little success in helping the young.

All three approaches emerged as responses to the needs and the particular labour market failures of the traditional industrial economies. They take a top-down approach that treats unemployment and the labour markets themselves as macro phenomena. Their success depends on the existence of large groups of relatively homogeneous workers suffering mass unemployment in the downswings of the business cycle, whose upswings take them up again when healthy growth resumes. When these conditions still reigned predominantly, the insertion of new, young workers into the employment system occurred relatively easily, practically as a rite of passage. Older workers threatened by technological change could be retrained and thus kept within the system. Public education and training were well adapted to the economy's requirements.

This book does not assert that all these public programmes should be scrapped. It has a much sharper focus, specifically on youth unemployment and the role that more solid encouragement of entrepreneurship among the young might play in alleviating this increasingly intractable problem. The changes in business organisation, workplace practices and skill requirements now sweeping across all of the industrial economies leave the young manifestly not helped by the traditional policies. Rising, longer-term youth unemployment and semi-employment in the midst of strong economic growth attest to that. Adaptations of the traditional policies *for this particular group* require a much more "micro" approach, geared to the variety and complexity of the new skill and work-habit requirements and clearly recognising the fragmentation and absence of homogeneity in the young labour force and the jobs potentially available for it.

One clear insight that emerged from the Rome conference was that effective re-integration of the young into the active labour force will in fact equip them with precisely those talents and skills that make for successful entrepreneurship. It follows, therefore, that policies to promote youth entrepreneurship need not be seen as a departure from the broad policy orientation needed in any case. Instead, programmes to train young people for self-employment and help them to achieve it can enhance what must be done to attack youth unemployment in general. Not all such people will want or adapt well to entrepreneurial careers. Yet those who do, in numbers greater than most policy makers now sus-

© OECD 2001

pect, can become a potent source of economic dynamism and more job creation, the ultimate goal.

Another sign of the failure of traditional systems to cure long-term unemployment in general and youth unemployment in particular lies in the industrial economies' burgeoning informal economies. Rather than remaining idle, and often spurred by perverse tax incentives, many of the long-term unemployed strike out on their own, outside the system, to operate in the underground economy. This phenomenon's implication for the thesis argued in this book lies in its demonstration that entrepreneurial urges and talents are indeed far more pervasive in ordinary persons than people conventionally realise. This writer has personal experience of a young family friend in France, with limited education but good manual skills, now in his mid-30s, who passed through a depressing unemployment experience in the 1990s. He found underground, independent artisan work for a time, and now has become the proud proprietor of a legitimate, registered, successful, tax-paying business. He has rescued himself from professional oblivion and regained his dignity. His young firm provides a living for him, his family and a business partner, as well as part-time work for occasional assistants. The OECD area has millions potentially like him.

Towards a definition of self-employment

The speakers at the Rome conference – all experts – discussed youth entrepreneurship more or less as if everyone understood what it meant. This produced a certain definitional elasticity that led to some incompatibility in the data presented and a tendency, as perceived by both the audience and the speakers themselves, to stray from the subject. Early discussions in a relatively new field often have these characteristics, which do not necessarily constitute a flaw and may actually help to solidify concepts. Because this book aims towards at least tentative, credible suggestions for policy, however, it needs more definitional rigour. Without it, policy targets cannot be well identified and policies themselves cannot be precisely crafted.

Broadly speaking, "entrepreneurship" is used synonymously with "self-employment". This defines an entrepreneur as anyone who works for himself or herself but not for someone else, except under arm's-length contracts or their conceptual equivalent. The definition includes those who work alone – at home, from a workshop-truck or in separate business premises[10] – as well as the owners of businesses with partners and/or employees. It embraces an enormous range of activities, from the humble to the exotic: artisans, craft and other manufacturers, writers, consultants, shopkeepers small and large, new Internet marketers and the famous "new-age" start-ups, favourites of the venture capitalists and frequently the brainchildren of what seem like barely weaned youngsters. Education, which this book covers in some depth in Chapter 3, plays an enormous role in where a self-employed person will find a place on this spectrum. It always will. Yet educational reforms, stressing multiple skills, flexibility, creativity and the proficiencies essential to entrepreneurship itself, can go far towards breaking down the class distinctions born of the industrial age and its typical employment patterns. They thus can free potential young entrepreneurs to see broader horizons in a world of rapid economic and social change.[11]

What about agriculture? Should family farms with and without hired hands, in some respects the earliest and best examples of entrepreneurial activity, be included in the definition for the purposes of this analysis and its eventual policy suggestions? Although the arguments for their inclusion are strong – and farmers certainly should never be forgotten as exemplars of entrepreneurial behaviour – they are excluded here, chiefly to focus the analysis and make it more manageable. This avoids complications that consideration of agriculture introduces:

- Rural populations are deeply affected by demographic changes associated with economic progress, chiefly migration from rural to urban areas. OECD countries are highly diverse in this respect. Some have largely completed such population shifts, others are in the midst of them and still others remain at relatively early stages. If one counts family farmers with other entrepreneurs and then attempts to compare, say, Turkey or Greece with France or the United Kingdom, the numbers simply reflect the proportions of working populations which remain rural and provide very poor measures of the incidence of entrepreneurial activity in the non-farm populations.
- Employment policy for farmers remains the domain of agricultural policy, which has problems, objectives and techniques (*e.g.*, subsidies on output) that differ so widely from those of non-farm labour policy that they merit separate rather than combined study. This applies especially to the entrepreneurial aspects of rural

life. Most OECD-area agricultural policies have for many decades given special attention to preserving the livelihoods of independent farmers, for historical, political and cultural reasons. Yet these policies have little to do with – and even can contrast with – the support needs of an urban labour force, including its entrepreneurs.

Nevertheless, the exclusion of farmer-entrepreneurs from this analysis does risk unavoidably missing some elements of interest, which should at least be highlighted here. Consider, for example, the family farm that may grow over time into an "industrial farm" with considerable employed labour and many of the organisational trappings of a non-farm business. At the other end of the spectrum, small farmers, too, feel the tug of modern marketing technology and act in entrepreneurial ways that really are germane to this inquiry. France, Italy and other European countries have many small "boutique" food-processing and marketing extensions of traditional family farming. The Internet may unleash them. They are, on any definition, real entrepreneurial businesses.

The state of entrepreneurship and attitudes towards it in the OECD area[12]

Before looking at what might be done to boost entrepreneurial initiatives among the young, it will help to have some understanding of the role that self-employment now plays for the collective and individual workforces of the OECD area, and of how that role has developed over the decades. Is entrepreneurship a waxing or a waning force in the OECD economies? Beyond that, what can be said about social attitudes towards self-employment, especially among younger members of the labour force? Fortunately, and although they are more than a decade old, some survey data are available to cast light on the latter question.

The setting

The Blanchflower and Oswald (1999) data on the self-employed in 22 OECD Member countries are gathered and analysed in Table 2 on the following page. The table presents the numbers of self-employed as a percentage of the working-age (18-64) population, and compares them over a bit more than two and a half decades, from 1970 to 1996. Excluding Turkey, for which data for 1970 are not available, average self-employment, agricultural and non-agricultural, in these 22 countries dropped from

Table 2. **A numerical survey of self-employment in the OECD area, 1970 and 1996**
(Self-employed, estimated, as a per cent of the population aged 18-64)

	All self-employed		Self-employed in agriculture		Self-employed outside agriculture	
	1970	1996	1970	1996	1970	1996
Australia	10.3	10.3	3.7	2.0	6.6	8.3
Austria	17.4	9.4[1]	10.8	1.1[1]	6.6	5.1[1]
Belgium	11.8	10.3[2]	2.7	1.1[2]	9.1	9.2[2]
Canada	7.8	7.6	3.5	1.4	4.3	6.2
Denmark	14.9	6.9	6.3	1.6	8.6	5.3
Finland	18.5	8.8	14.7	3.1	3.8	5.7
France	14.2	6.5	7.1	1.9	7.1	4.6
Germany	11.3	6.7[3]	5.0	1.2[3]	6.3	5.5[3]
Greece	28.8[4]	25.0[3]	n.a.	10.5[3]	n.a.	14.5
Iceland	11.8	14.8	6.6	3.4	5.2	11.4
Ireland	19.5	11.7	14.6	7.2	4.9	4.5
Italy	19.6	14.7[1]	8.1	2.3[1]	11.5	12.4[1]
Japan	24.3	13.5[3]	11.4	3.6	12.9	9.9
Luxembourg	12.1	5.8[3]	5.3	1.5	6.8	4.3
Netherlands	9.0	8.2	3.0	1.3	6.0	6.9
New Zealand	9.0	14.4	5.0	3.7	4.0	10.7
Norway	12.4	6.5	7.7	2.4	4.7	4.1
Portugal	17.7	19.1	10.9	6.4	6.8	12.7
Spain	20.4	11.6	11.9	2.7	8.5	8.9
Sweden	8.1	7.6	3.9	1.3	4.2	3.7
Turkey	n.a.	30.6	n.a.	22.5	n.a.	8.1
United Kingdom	7.0	6.1	2.0	0.9	5.0	5.2
Summary statistics:						
Average	14.1	11.5	6.9	3.8	6.7	9.2
Average (excl. Turkey)	14.1	10.7	6.9	2.9	6.7	9.3
Median	12.1	11.6	6.3	2.4	6.6	8.3

1. Data are for 1994.
2. Data are for 1993.
3. Data are for 1995.
4. Data are for 1969.
The averages are unweighted.
Source and Methodology: The table is based on Tables 1 and 2 in Blanchflower and Oswald (1999), with data originally from the OECD *Labour Force Statistics*, various issues. The 1970 All self-employed values are based on interpolation between known 1966 and 1976 values. The 1996 value for self-employed in agriculture is derived from an extrapolation of 1970-95 data.

14.1 per cent to 10.7 per cent of the working-age population. Taking account of substantial declines in agriculture due to rural-urban migration, however, estimated self-employment outside agriculture – of main interest here – actually rose fairly significantly, to 9.3 per cent from 6.7 per cent of the growing working-age population, over these 26 years.

Thus, on average, non-farm self-employment is indeed expanding, modestly but solidly, compared to wage-earning labour. It will almost certainly pass through ten per cent of the active labour force in the present decade, if it has not done so already.

The averages nevertheless hide substantial variations among the 22 countries. The wide range of values for non-agricultural self-employment narrowed only slightly over the 26 years. It reached from 3.8 per cent to 12.9 per cent of the active population in 1970 and from 3.7 per cent to 11.4 per cent in 1996 (omitting the 14.5% in Greece, which did not have comparable data for both years). The values also actually fell in nine of the 22 remaining countries – Austria, Denmark, France, Germany, Ireland, Japan, Luxembourg, Norway and Sweden. Clearly, individual national situations vary considerably in their encouragement of entrepreneurial activity.

A *deeper look*

Several of the papers related to the Rome Conference support a deeper examination of the current self-employment setting in some of the OECD Member countries. The most comprehensive of them (Belussi, 1999) covers *Italy* in detail. It describes the Italian labour market as undergoing major changes, characterised less by an expansion of the country's traditionally high levels of self-employment than by the emergence of what Belussi calls "second-generation" self-employment built around new forms of independent work.

Citing data from the same source used by Blanchflower and Oswald (1999),[13] Belussi (1999) begins by confirming Italy's high and rising self-employment relative to the other large European economies (Table 3). Indeed, these figures suggest levels considerably higher within the *working* population than the estimates in Table 2, which compare the self-employed with the total working-age population.[14] The key figures from the point of view of this book cover manufacturing and services, where 4.3 million people, 23.0 per cent of the working labour force in these sectors combined, were self-employed in 1996, as against 3.3 million (19.2%) in 1980. The selected international comparisons in the table show Italy clearly in the lead, although the proportions of self-employed in these sectors grew somewhat more rapidly in Germany and spectacularly faster (by 72%) in the United Kingdom.

Table 3. **Self-employment in Italy, 1980-1996, with some international comparisons**
(Per cent of employment that is self-employment[1] in each sectoral grouping)

	1980	1985	1990	1996
Italy:				
Total economy	23.2	24.3	24.5	24.8
Agriculture[2]	47.6	47.8	47.9	49.8
Non-agriculture:[3]				
Italy	19.2	21.3	22.2	23.0
United Kingdom	7.1	. .	. .	12.2
Germany	8.7	. .	. .	10.6
Spain	16.2	. .	. .	18.5

1. Defined as employers and persons working on their own account.
2. Includes hunting, forestry and fishing.
3. Manufacturing and services combined.
Source: Belussi (1999), Table 1, based on OECD *Labour Force Statistics*, 1997.

These developments highlight three factors. First, self-employment has reinforced economic flexibility and contributed to a more efficient allocation of resources. Second, and focusing now on the most efficient parts of the Italian economy, in its characteristic industrial clusters and the regions marked by the development of small firms, the labour market appears to have adapted quite well to the emergence of flexible production systems and advanced methods of production management. Third, high rates of turbulence (in firm start-ups and closures, changes in the legal form of businesses, mergers and acquisitions and outsourcing arrangements) have increased the risks of job displacement and have accelerated labour mobility.

Because self-employment is such an important traditional feature of the Italian economy, the statistical agency, ISTAT, has collected survey data that permit insights from a detailed breakdown of people *within* the general category of self-employment. Belussi's analysis of these data is pulled together in Table 4. The ISTAT figures break self-employment into five categories: entrepreneurs, professionals, autonomous workers (the dominant group, which includes shopkeepers, artisans and farmers), co-operative workers and working family members. They show significant growth among independent professionals and entrepreneurs in the decade and a half from 1980 to 1995.

Table 4. **Civil employment in Italy by professional status, 1980 and 1995**
(Numbers of persons in thousands and percentages of totals at the bottom of each column)

Professional status	Manufacturing				Building and construction				Other sectors				Total			
	1980		1995		1980		1995		1980		1995		1980		1995	
	No.	%	No.	%	No.	%	No.	%	No.	%	No.	%	No.	%	No.	%
Entrepreneurs	43	0.8	100	2.2	56	2.7	73	4.5	57	0.4	194	1.4	156	0.7	367	1.8
Professional workers	21	0.4	30	0.6	28	1.4	55	3.4	263	2.0	626	4.5	312	1.5	711	3.6
Autonomous workers	462	8.4	344	7.4	285	13.8	413	25.6	3 157	24.1	2 859	20.8	3 904	18.9	3 616	18.1
Co-operative workers	41	0.7	39	0.8	25	1.2	17	1.0	1 040	7.9	172	1.3	1 046	5.1	228	1.1
Working family members	92	1.7	74	1.6	21	1.0	40	2.5	74	0.6	736	5.3	339	1.9	850	4.2
Self-employed	660	12.1	587	12.7	415	20.1	598	37.0	5 302	40.4	4 585	33.3	5 277	28.0	5 770	28.8
Employees	4 803	87.9	4 036	87.3	1 645	79.9	1 017	63.0	9 099	69.6	9 186	66.7	14 828	72.0	14 239	71.2
Total	5 463	100.0	4 623	100.0	2 060	100.0	1 615	100.0	13 081	100.0	13 771	100.0	20 604	100.0	20 009	100.0

Source: Belussi (1999), Tables 2 and 3. Based on ISTAT data and analysis in Rapiti (1997).

According to Belussi (1999), the large group of autonomous workers reflects varying influences. Overall, its share has declined somewhat, but in building and construction it has expanded sharply as heavier use of sub-contractors has gained more than a foothold in this sector. Manufacturing shows apparently contrasting influences. Small artisan enterprises have gone out of business in declining areas, but a strong pattern of small-firm creation persists in the more dynamic areas and, most important, the number of wage employees in the artisan sub-sector has expanded dramatically. In the past decade, manufacturing firms with fewer than 19 employees have mushroomed, giving the sub-sector a significant share of total wage employment. These developments thus reveal not only the expansion of flexible self-employment as a generator of wage jobs (*i.e.*, more self-employed professionals and entrepreneurs, who hire more help) but also a striking shift in wage-labour demand towards less-protected working conditions and non-unionised shops.

The "autonomous" group still claimed two out of every three self-employed workers in 1995. Belussi notes that Sestito (1989) provides several plausible explanations for its strength. They include the diminishing role of scale economies, tax advantages (which were reduced in 1985, however), a tendency for self-employment to mask unemployment during cyclical downturns, the relative advantages of small firms in managing turbulent industrial relations and demand instability.

Belussi also looks at labour flows, particularly the frequency and intensity of entry into and exit from self-employment. The paper hypothesises the following sequence: "*New entries occur in both self-employment and the wage sectors, but the most relevant flows are those from unemployment into wage sectors. A significant share (10 people out of 100) . . . of new self-employment comes from wage labour. The change of status from dependent jobs to self-employment describes the typical Italian mechanism through which new firms are created.*" (Belussi, 1997, p. 7) Supporting analysis comes from Contini and Pacelli (1995), which not only found mobility flows more significant than previously supposed, but also estimated the characteristics of the wage workers most likely to enter self-employment. The highest probabilities of such shifts were associated with prior employment in industry or commerce, white-collar workers, people between 21 and 35 years old (note the youth element here) and prior jobs in firms in the eastern part of Italy with fewer than 20 employees.

Belussi stresses the perils of using aggregate self-employment figures alone to understand the many changes that have occurred, a lesson applicable to all countries. "*On the one hand, in sectors where self-employment was very important traditionally (agriculture and commerce), there has been a process of rationalisation and restructuring, so the share of self-employment has decreased relatively (but not in the emerging ... tertiary activities based on communications and information services). On the other hand, in manufacturing and construction, sectors where self-employment was relatively low, and was supposed to be declining, there has been a sudden upsurge, thanks to the impact of outsourcing, industrial restructuring, subcontracting and economic decentralisation.*" (Belussi, 1999, p. 8.)

Moreover, a new group has emerged, performing "a-typical" work, a mix between self-employment and wage work; in Italy, it is regulated by a special type of contract. At one extreme, such work – *e.g.*, in some subcontracting situations – can leave the "entrepreneur" only nominally independent, tied to a single client and squeezed unmercifully by pricing pressures and severe tasking. More generally, a *continuum* of situations has emerged between the solid old categories of "firms" and "employees", along which people function with varying degrees of entrepreneurial autonomy and market freedom.

The *United Kingdom* is Europe's second most entrepreneurial large economy, and has by far the fastest-growing self-employment rates. According to Irwin (1999), more than a third of the nation's young people express a desire to start their own businesses, and each year about 50 000 of them actually do it. In the labour market as a whole, self-employment rose from 9 per cent in 1981 to 13 per cent in 1996; the numbers of self-employed peaked at 3.57 million in 1990, but have fallen back to around 3.3 million currently. Within that population, the 16-24 age cohort has the lowest self-employment rate (3.3%) and people over 65 the highest (36%) – but the numerical majority among the millions of self-employed people is between 25 and 44 years old.

Irwin (1999) cites other evidence, specifically related to young entrepreneurs, from a 1997 Barclays Bank survey. The source of the estimate mentioned above of 50 000 new, young entrepreneurs (aged 18-24) annually, this survey found "a flourishing youth-enterprise culture" in the United Kingdom. Some 45 per cent of these new proprietors are female. Sixty-five per cent work from their homes, 40 per cent work alone, 14 per cent have a single employee and about 17 per cent employ six or more people. Most of these businesses (71%) have an annual turnover of under £100 000 ($158 000, €163 000),[15] but about 10 per cent are significantly larger. It cost entrepreneurs under age 25 about £5 000 ($7 900, €8 200) to set up their businesses, although the average cost of all new-business formations in 1997 was £11 000

($17 400, €18 000). Somewhat more than half (53%) of the founders left full-time employment to establish their enterprises, while only 10 per cent came from unemployment. Most of the rest came directly from schooling or were otherwise not previously in the labour force. According to another source, graduates, motivated primarily by desires for independence and flexibility rather than either job security or riches, form an important source of new entrepreneurs (Tackey and Perryman, 1999). This analysis found about 12 per cent of graduates in self-employment a year after finishing their schooling and about 15 per cent in their own businesses two years later.

The paper on *France* presented by Philippe Salles at the Rome conference (Salles, 1999) begins somewhat pessimistically, speaking of the country's "fragile basis" for entrepreneurship in general and youth entrepreneurship in particular. During the 1990s, new-business creations in France dropped steadily, from an estimated 312 000 in 1989 to 276 000 in 1991, 275 000 in 1996, 272 000 in 1997 and 267 000 in 1998, before rising slightly to 269 000 in 1999. At least two factors temper the implications of these figures somewhat, however. First, they are not net numbers. In fact, they more or less compensate for business failures, which are dropping sharply, so the "population" of young firms probably holds up better, on balance. Second, new-firm formation has diversified towards sectors with a strong development potential. Moreover, what one might characterise as "greenfield" start-ups – brand-new enterprises as opposed to, for example, restarts by artisans who go in and out of business – have shown somewhat more strength and more volatility as well. From a peak of 206 000 in 1989, they fell to 171 000 in 1993, climbed to 184 000 in 1994, then declined gently to 166 000 in 1998 before rising again (twice as much as the overall figure) to 170 000 in 1999.

Salles (1999) attributes the relatively lacklustre entrepreneurial performance in France primarily to a lack of public awakening to a "spirit of enterprise", especially among the young. France's relatively slow economic growth during most of the 1990s (a real recovery did not begin to take off until late in the decade), as well as a decline in official financial support for new entrepreneurs – which is reviving again under new programmes (see Chapter 2) – served as contributing factors. Like Serieyx (1998), the Salles paper takes a deeply critical view of the French education system, citing its (and society's) excessive valuation of formal educational credentials and suppression of entrepreneurial training. This has two results. First, the best educated become the least entrepreneurial. During the

© OECD 2001

mid-1990s, for example, only 6 per cent of France's graduate engineers created their own firms, and did so late, after long periods of salaried employment. Second, and at the other extreme, among young people with lesser qualifications, a sort of socially induced "self-censure" operates against their going into business for themselves, along with no encouragement from the social workers and similar people with whom they may come into contact and by whom they might otherwise be influenced more positively.

These public views may be changing, perhaps in the wake of France's now stronger economic performance and from the force of ideas at high levels, like the Chirac quote that began this book. Salles (1999) notes two key pieces of survey information that suggest such change. In an IFOP/APCE survey of March 1998, 1.2 million French people (versus 700 000 in a 1992 survey) had definite plans to begin or re-found their own businesses, and 32 per cent of them intended to do so before a year had passed. MENRT/SOFRES did a survey in January 1999, directed specifically at beginning and finishing secondary (*lycée*) students as well as those in the first year of study for a BTS (B*revet de Technicien Supérieur*, a professional qualification equal to the BAC plus two additional years of technical study). It found 32 per cent of the respondents seriously envisaging the creation of an enterprise as their first professional track. Many of these intentions must indeed translate into reality. New enterprises in 1998 created some 530 000 new jobs. Those seeking employees represented 40 per cent of the new firms that came into existence, thus illustrating what Salles characterises as the "virtuous circle" of enterprise and employment creation.

In *Canada*, Grant and Dupuy (1999) note that the proportion of the self-employed among people with jobs jumped to 16.6 per cent in 1996 from 13.8 per cent in 1989, which suggests growth about five times as fast as in Italy over the period. The authors cite three other studies (Gauthier and Roy, 1997; Picot, Manser and Lin, 1998; Lin, Picot and Yates, 1999), which say that about 80 per cent of Canada's net employment gains during the 1990s came from self-employment. Outside agriculture, where self-employment of course dominates, construction and business services had the highest self-employment rates (35% and 32%) as well as their fastest 1989-96 growth (33% and 21%). In the same period, self-employment among Canada's youth (aged 15-24) rose rapidly as well. In 1996, it reached 7 per cent of all employed workers in the age group, up from 5.4 per cent in 1989.

Table 5. **Youth and self-employment in Australia, 1995**

Sector	Numbers of self-employed[1]		Persons 15-24 as per cent of:	
	All ages	Age 15-24	15-24 group	Sector total
Total	1 189 576	56 081	100.0	4.7
less: Agriculture[2]	–225 848	–4 233	7.5	1.9
Total, outside agriculture	963 728	51 848	100.0	5.4
Construction	200 187	15 730	30.3	7.1
Personal and other services	61 652	7 161	13.8	11.6
Retail trade	203 867	6 70L7	12.9	3.3
Property and business services	143 588	5 764	11.1	4.0
Manufacturing	70 157	3 425	6.6	4.9
Mining	2 902	317	5.6	10.9
Education	16 206	2 647	5.1	8.1
Health and community services	32 413	2 628	5.1	8.1
Transport and storage	63 625	2 235	4.3	3.5
Wholesale trade	40 378	1 754	3.3	4.1
Accommodation, cafes, restaurants	36 102	1 395	2.7	3.9
Finance and insurance	9 295	395	0.8	4.2
Communication services	10 447	350	0.7	3.4
Others	485	0	0	0

1. These figures contain a high degree of standard error because they are based on weighted estimates of quarterly samples.
2. Agriculture includes forestry and fishing.
Source: White (1999), page 7, based on ABS, *Labour Force Survey* 1995, Canberra.

For *Australia*, while White (1999) does not describe the self-employment setting in full detail or in the same way, he does provide some 1995 figures, with useful sectoral breakdowns, on the degree to which young people participate in their country's enterprise culture (Table 5). Outside agriculture, where young independent farmers are much rarer relative to their older counterparts than are young entrepreneurs in non-farm occupations, some 5 per cent – 5.5 per cent of the self-employed, on average, are between 15 and 24 years old. Almost 70 per cent of them appear in four sub-sectors, construction, personal and other services, retail trade and property and business services. Their penetration rate (share of self-employment in each sub-sector) lies above the average in the first two, but below it in the second two. Although their numbers are not very large (just over ten per cent of the self-employed in their age group), young people – women more than men – account for relatively high proportions of the self-employed of all ages in both education and health, and community services. Except in the category of personal and other services, the 15-19 age group plays only a small role in all of these figures, which those aged 20-24 dominate. Generally, young men are more likely than young women to be self-employed. White (1999) also reports, from a separate survey, the following additional characteristics of respondents among Australia's young entrepreneurs:

- Most had completed secondary education, and the highest educational credentials of many were high-school certificates, TAFE certificates or, sometimes, completed apprenticeships.
- Most operated as sole traders.
- Most struggled to generate sufficient revenues; slightly more than half had turnover of less than A$1 000 (US$610, €632) per month.
- Two-thirds of them operated from their homes and most had no employees.

Attitudes

Survey evidence from 1989 for 11 countries, including eight of those considered above, strongly suggests that many more people in all age groups, and particularly younger workers, would like to run their own businesses or work in the smaller firms typical of entrepreneurial start-ups. Table 6 shows that remarkably high proportions of survey respondents express preferences for self-employment and for working in small rather than large firms. Among those under 30 years of age, only the Netherlands and Norway showed fewer than 50 per cent of respondents preferring self-employment, and only in Italy did fewer than half prefer small workplaces over large ones. Assuming that questionnaire material can be viewed as reliable, a large, latent demand exists for entrepreneurial work. People find self-employment intrinsically attractive.

Other survey data cited by Blanchflower and Oswald (1999) try to measure differences in the skills and other relevant attributes of the employed and self-employed. A special 1990 Eurobarometer Survey[16] of 7 706 people aged 15-24 in the 15 EU countries found that about a third of them said they could use computers or word processors very well or fairly well, but that the self-employed among them were less skilled in this respect than those who were employees. In general, the self-employed in this sample got less training than employees and tended more than

Table 6. **Some survey results on workplace preferences, 1989**
(Per cent of respondents, given a hypothetical choice, preferring self-employment and small over large firms)

	All ages		Under 30 years of age	
	Per cent	No. of respondents	Per cent	No. of respondents
A. Those preferring self-employment				
Austria	60.20	1 779	64.10	482
Great Britain	47.75	1 183	51.78	245
Hungary	38.03	894	54.22	201
Ireland	50.95	944	50.44	226
Israel	48.57	910	59.02	327
Italy	65.22	969	72.76	246
Netherlands	38.54	1 489	40.29	412
Northern Ireland	51.52	705	58.21	144
Norway	26.05	1 589	31.68	464
United States	62.97	1 283	66.31	285
Germany (West)	49.04	1 207	59.60	251
B. Those preferring small over large firms				
Austria	65.67	1 646	71.20	455
Great Britain	71.61	1 102	62.69	219
Hungary	59.30	892	65.51	203
Ireland	65.69	892	56.48	216
Israel	52.48	806	52.08	288
Italy	46.57	904	40.59	234
Netherlands	73.76	1 372	68.51	378
Northern Ireland	64.63	638	60.05	138
Norway	76.12	1 470	76.87	441
United States	61.11	1 219	51.07	278
Germany (West)	56.14	1 214	51.35	248

Source: From Blanchflower and Oswald (1999); original data from International Social Survey Programme, 1989.

employees to find their work through families and friends. They also expressed noticeably more satisfaction with their work. The information on computer skills is highly suspect because it is old. Young people have developed these skills rapidly and in far greater numbers over the past decade. Nevertheless, both this information and the results on training in general tend to confirm a suggestion made earlier – that the potential entrepreneurs in our societies are not always the technologically adept and better -educated, as romantic popular notions might suggest.

The question of differences in job satisfaction between the employed and the self-employed deserves further investigation because

Table 7. **Job satisfaction**
(Per cent of people with work reporting satisfaction at various levels)

	Not at all satisfied	Not very satisfied	Fairly satisfied	Very satisfied	Number of respondents
A. Employees					
Belgium	0.97	5.97	51.58	41.48	775
Denmark	1.83	3.70	5.42	49.06	919
Germany (West)	4.68	10.97	52.40	31.95	889
Germany (East)	2.05	8.57	56.61	32.77	927
Greece	6.37	25.22	55.59	12.82	526
Italy	5.12	18.31	56.95	19.62	727
Spain	4.04	16.76	56.65	22.55	757
France	4.69	13.81	61.01	20.49	862
Ireland	1.13	4.82	39.33	54.72	775
Luxembourg	2.41	5.75	56.62	35.22	418
Netherlands	1.42	7.24	46.92	44.41	962
Portugal	3.30	13.54	62.27	20.89	696
Great Britain	4.69	9.28	49.07	36.96	925
Finland	1.55	5.18	62.75	30.52	903
Sweden	2.48	5.71	54.74	37.07	967
Austria	1.49	9.29	46.51	42.71	937
Euro 15	12	11.75	54.04	30.17	12 965
B. Self-employed					
Belgium	0.39	4.56	39.34	54.13	233
Denmark	0.00	0.00	5.42	60.66	73
Germany (West)	1.69	10.81	38.90	48.60	135
Germany (East)	2.02	8.17	48.50	41.31	119
Greece	13.09	33.64	43.55	9.73	476
Italy	1.76	6.81	52.81	38.62	301
Spain	3.02	13.65	57.55	25.78	239
France	8.03	11.80	51.96	28.21	126
Ireland	0.41	1.72	31.36	66.51	229
Luxembourg	1.49	1.92	34.23	62.36	71
Netherlands	1.13	0.79	39.48	58.60	101
Portugal	1.86	13.54	62.97	22.69	299
Great Britain	2.60	4.13	47.40	45.87	137
Finland	2.24	10.10	55.81	31.84	150
Sweden	0.00	2.58	34.25	63.17	88
Austria	1.64	8.56	37.65	52.15	128
Euro 15	3.27	10.14	48.32	38.27	2 905

Note: All estimates are weighted.
Source: Eurobarometer (1996), *Working Conditions in the European Union*, No. 44.2, November 1995-January 1996.

answers to it shed much light on attitudes towardst entrepreneurial behaviour. Table 7 on the following page, based on much more recent information (1995-96), indicates clearly that self-employmenassociates with greater job

© OECD 2001

satisfaction among respondents in the EU countries. Taking these countries together, some 38 per cent of the self-employed respondents said they were "very satisfied" with their work, as against 30 per cent for the employees in the sample. Econometric tests, which included controls for occupation, industry, age, gender, job tenure, commuting time, firm size, education and the countries themselves, confirmed these results for both people of all working ages and those under 30 years old (see Blanchflower and Oswald, 1999, p. 6 and Table 6). At the other extreme, considerably fewer self-employed people than employees declared themselves "not at all" or "not very" satisfied in their work. In two countries, which paradoxically have not revealed themselves in the data presented so far as cultures especially prone to entrepreneurial ventures, zeroes (less than 0.005 per cent) actually appeared in these categories. Denmark and Sweden showed no completely unsatisfied self-employed persons, and Denmark came up with a zero in the "not very satisfied" column as well.

If people are more satisfied when they are self-employed, what are the elements on which they base this satisfaction? According to Blanchflower and Oswald (1999), people view their jobs as more than just a source of income. They care most about job security and interesting work, with the ability to work independently figuring quite strongly as well. These data do not permit much differentiation between the attitudes of younger and older people. Drawing on the Eurobarometer Surveys of 1975 to 1996, however, and using formal econometric analysis, the authors come up with the important result that young, self-employed people have higher "life satisfaction", other things equal, than others in the same age groups and with similar characteristics. Self-employed young men and women are unusually content with their lives.

Blanchflower and Oswald (1999) make a final effort to ascertain precisely what sorts of people actually become self-employed. In all countries, they find age and gender to be statistically associated with a greater probability of self-employment. Other things equal, older people and men are the more likely entrepreneurs. While young people are more likely to have positive attitudes towards self-employment, reality impedes them – a possible barrier that policy could overcome. Overall, the determinants of self-employment for the young and the old look very similar, even among finer age breakdowns for younger people. The probability of self-employment for the under-30 sample rises with age and

© OECD 2001

household size, is higher for men than for women and (in contrast to the older group) for married persons as opposed to single people. Some evidence also suggests that self-employment is highest for those with the least and those with the most education.

Concluding remarks

This chapter began by stressing the problem of youth unemployment as a key policy concern. A growing pool of jobless young people, especially if their plight becomes a long-term one and they eventually leave the labour force in despair, is not only unfortunate in itself but also a waste of resources that could otherwise contribute to the economy. The problem roots in the vast technological, structural and behavioural changes sweeping through the OECD area's workplaces. Evidence becomes clearer and clearer that it will not be solved on the unemployment-benefit dole queues or in labour offices designed to match factory workers with jobs in the industrial age.

Can policy makers find a solution in stronger promotion of youth entrepreneurship, *i.e.*, self-employment? Before beginning to seek an answer to that question, one must understand something about the nature of entrepreneurship in the industrial countries and about social attitudes towards it, especially among the young who would become the main targets of the new policies. On the evidence available over the decades up to about the mid-1990s, self-employment appears to be gaining some ground in the OECD economies, although not at a blistering rate in most of them. New jobs come with it, as entrepreneurs themselves become employers. The survey evidence just presented suggests further that self-employment brings direct microeconomic benefits to people. Self-employed individuals report markedly greater well being than comparable employees, in terms of job satisfaction, contented lives and general happiness with their situations. Moreover, younger workers are more prone than older ones to envision themselves in self-employment and to prefer smaller over larger establishments in which to work. Across the OECD area, many millions of employees, young and old, say that they would prefer to work for themselves. People, especially younger ones, look for jobs, entrepreneurial or not, that permit them to work independently. Finally, such self-employment as does exist would seem to be accessible to those with both the least and the most education.

© OECD 2001

Yet reality does not match these expectations. Why are not more individuals running their own businesses? Blanchflower and Oswald (1999) cite a convincing volume of empirical economic research that highlights a lack of start-up and working capital as a major constraint on founding new businesses.[17] Their own work reveals three aspects of the same phenomenon for the United Kingdom, and research by others has reached similar conclusions for the United States and Sweden:

- Most small businesses are begun with one's own or family money. Receiving money from inheritances or other sources is especially important for young entrepreneurs.
- Established entrepreneurs say that they needed more help with finance than with other aspects of creating their businesses.
- Where to obtain capital is the single biggest source of concern for potential entrepreneurs.

These findings all stop short of recommending programmes that provide capital or subsidised lending to new entrepreneurs. The authors confine themselves to identifying the issue, which is but one of many that policy makers need to consider for promoting entrepreneurship as a way of dealing with youth unemployment and the public and social costs it entails. The rest of this book explores them all.

Chapter 2

Emerging Programme Approaches to Youth Entrepreneurship

Introduction

No single policy model exists for the encouragement and promotion of entrepreneurial activity among younger people. Indeed, as new programmes develop in various national and cultural settings, they tend to show more, rather than less variety in their content and delivery mechanisms. This chapter tries to pull together an unwieldy mass of information about entrepreneurship programmes in different OECD Member countries, striving for a comparative approach. It seeks to identify underlying concepts useful for policy makers and others interested in practical action. It does not attempt a full inventory of programmes in any of the countries selected, but rather highlights those that have emerged as examples of "best practice" in various national settings.

To provide a foundation, Figure 3 looks schematically at two questions: "Who does this work?" and "What do the programmes entail?" The answers provide simply a menu of possibilities. In practice, their combinations take many forms. No country involves all the players and all the elements in any truly systematic way. Even to contemplate such an approach is probably utopian. For practical policy, however, Figure 3 does serve to indicate the broad ranges of players and activities that exist in one country or another, and to suggest to policy makers where gaps might be filled.

Conceptually, promoting entrepreneurship sometimes begins as early as in curricular or extra-curricular primary education, with acculturation through information and awareness-building programmes. Such activities also occur later as well. Most education that inculcates actual

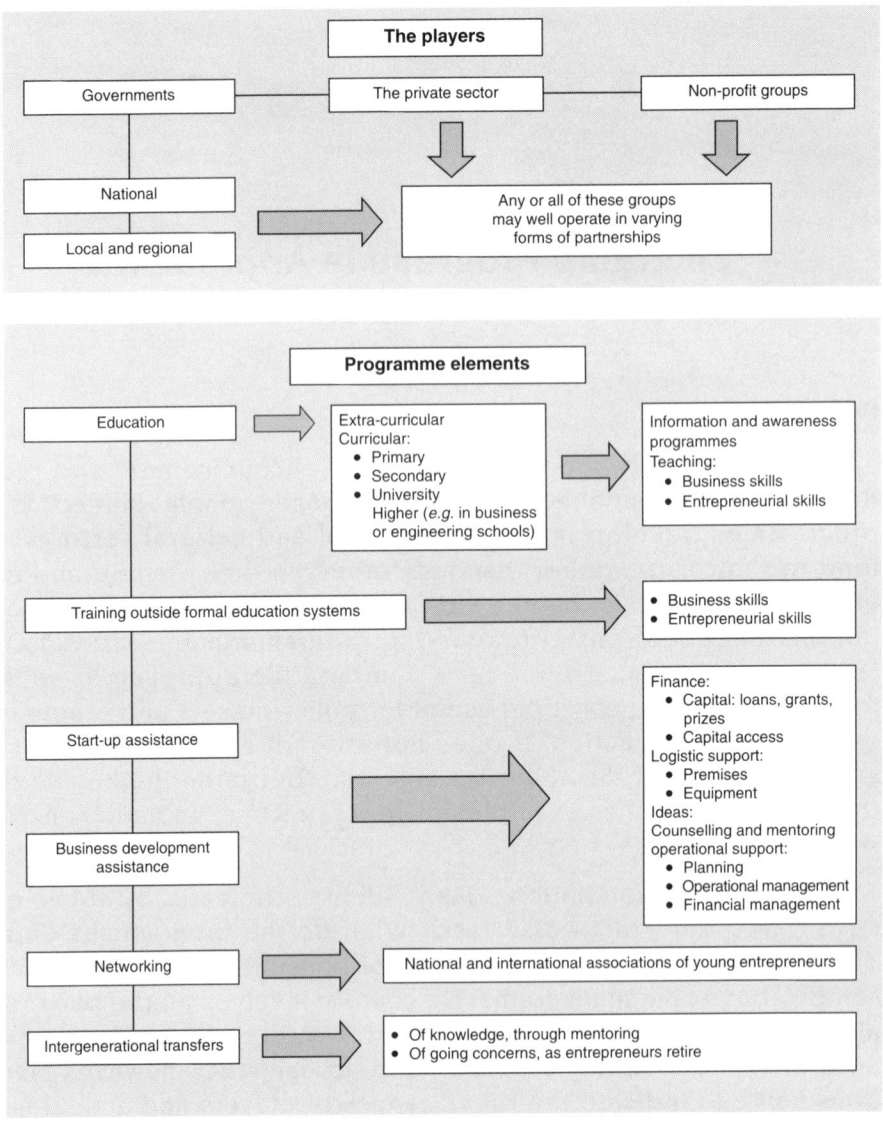

Source: OECD.

business and entrepreneurial skills intensifies progressively as people pass through their teenage years, go on into university, and seek still higher education. Training outside the educational system can either reinforce what occurs during schooling or fill gaps – often large ones – that most educational systems still leave open. Programmes geared primarily to start-up assistance must often provide such training. For those both trained and ready to establish their own businesses, the emphasis shifts to practical help for start-ups – access to capital, logistical support and operational assistance – and similar measures for young firms that have passed the start-up stage and are ready to expand. Mirroring how democratic societies and their business communities' work, young entrepreneurs may form associations both for mutual help and to represent their interests. Finally, some programmes pay attention to the potential for intergenerational transfers, chiefly of the knowledge that established entrepreneurs and business people can pass on if organised to do so (*e.g.*, through mentor programmes), but also of businesses themselves, as their proprietors retire.

While the foregoing description may seem fairly systematic, no country replicates it in full, with all relevant institutions pulling together to perform all the activities, in an ordered sequence and reaching entire populations. No country has an "entrepreneurship czar", and few, if any, would want one. Nevertheless, the logic of what is needed is sufficiently evident – and the OECD economies are sufficiently similar to reveal that logic in at least its broad outlines – that the many programmes surveyed all fall somewhere along the spectrum shown in Figure 3. From this perspective, the differences among countries hold the most interest and raise the key questions: To what degree do youth entrepreneurship programmes reach throughout the relevant youth populations? What are the respective roles of governmental and private entities in delivering these services? What do the programme emphases reveal about national perceptions of where such services are most needed?

Many experts in the field believe passionately that entrepreneurial education and training should begin as early as possible, for two main reasons. First, they obviously form an essential component of the preparation of potential young entrepreneurs to go into business for themselves. Second, they also instil entrepreneurial habits of mind and work skills that can serve just as well for successful employees in the new,

© OECD 2001

globalised, post-industrial economy as for those who actually choose to establish their own enterprises. As the country analyses in this chapter will show, many programmes closely link education and training with other forms of assistance. Although they really cannot be separated from these other kinds of help, however, their role has been deemed sufficiently important that the following chapter will explore it in detail. These processes of acculturation and imparting flexible capabilities, important as they are, take time, and concern long-term as well as short-term policy. Their effects often reveal themselves slowly rather than immediately. Countries seeking seriously to boost youth entrepreneurship in the short term, to reduce unemployment and adapt to the emerging economy, need and want quicker results. They tend, therefore, to put more immediate policy emphasis on programmes for start-up and business-development support, often including special training outside the educational system to fill skill gaps ignored by traditional education.

As the discussion in Chapter I showed, perhaps the largest single barrier to establishment for any entrepreneur, and especially for younger ones, lies in finding sufficient start-up and working capital to see a business successfully through its initial stages. This controversial subject risks entanglement in a sterile debate over whether or not governments should subsidise the formation of young businesses or provide loan guarantees that have a subsidy effect if they provide capital at below-market interest rates. Many governments are willing to intervene in these ways; some are not. Some successful privately financed programmes, although they have limited resources and surely do not reach all potential young entrepreneurs, use loans, grants and prizes as sources of capital for new, young firms. Outside the purview of formal programmes, many young people continue to find their initial capital in the traditional, not always egalitarian ways – through inheritances or loans from family and friends.

The problem of young entrepreneurs' *access* to capital has just as much importance as the supply of capital itself. It can represent a formidable barrier to new-business formation, even in rich and growing economies. It has two aspects. On the one hand, bankers and other lenders or investors (*e.g.*, venture capitalists) may share a general social bias, which doubts the capability of younger people to found businesses successfully. Perhaps partly because of this, and certainly because young entrepreneurs remain a relatively rare breed, potential lenders can themselves have education and training gaps; they often are incapable of properly evaluating viable youth-business proposals. Some signs point to a change for the better in this respect. Many successful programmes associate bankers closely with their work, and bankers even have established a few of them. On the other hand, a recurrent theme in numerous public and private youth-entrepreneurship programmes across the OECD area closely links the young businessperson's ability to prepare adequate business plans to other forms of start-up assistance. Without a good business plan, the search for capital becomes justifiably hopeless. Programme operators most commonly make their help conditional on the preparation of such plans, often after appropriate training. With a good plan, the programme operator can effectively proceed to help the young entrepreneur try to find a willing lender, or can provide the capital if the programme has that capability.

Whether or not they provide or help with finding capital, many programmes offer other kinds of start-up and business-development support, in an attempt to make their approaches to aiding young entrepreneurs as holistic as possible. Perhaps the most common such services involve generalised counselling and mentoring before and after young business form. In one way or another, they often enlist the help of experienced, sometimes retired businessmen, who work closely with the new firms. Programmes often provide payment for such work. Other services have a more operational focus, giving help with ongoing planning, operational and financial management (*e.g.*, accounting), and some will furnish the young business person with temporary initial premises, display space and the like. Some private business donors are willing to make available free or low-cost equipment, such as servers, PCs and software for networked computer systems.

There is one common gap, however. Except in just a few countries and programmes, continued assistance for business development and expansion after a year or so of operations remains almost absent. This may occur because official programmes and even some private ones become biased by short-term labour-policy issues, namely reducing youth unemployment and the associated social problems quickly and sharply. Yet the potential for new businesses to generate new jobs as they grow and hire may in fact appear most strongly as they get beyond

© OECD 2001

the throes of initial establishment. From a policy perspective, therefore, the absence of business-development and expansion programmes for young entrepreneurs may represent a significant lost opportunity.

To sum up so far, the impediments to successful self-employment for younger people lie partly in their lack of awareness of its potential, partly in their lack of appropriate education and training, and partly in practical issues of getting started in their own businesses, surviving and growing. Programmes to remedy these impediments all cover one or more of these three factors, but with much variation in goals, objectives and techniques. They take essentially three steps, which are not hierarchical but equal in importance. The first, to raise awareness that business creation and self-employment are viable career options, encourages such attitudinal change through role models and information services. It may have a short-term focus, when it tries to reach potential young entrepreneurs in age groups appropriate for enterprise establishment, or a long-term one, in programmes (usually extra-curricular) aimed at the very young. The second, a long-term approach, enhances learning and the weight of teaching business and entrepreneurial skills within or parallel with the education system at all levels. The third, a shift back to short-term goals, provides actual start-up and business-support services.

Some comparative country surveys

Italy[18]

The Italian school system has no focus on entrepreneurial education and not much internal debate about improving it. Yet, paradoxically, the country has gained recognition as a leader in fostering enterprise development and creating mechanisms that spread technical knowledge and generate real economic growth. The evidence presented in Chapter I indicated clearly that Italy has exceptionally high self-employment rates and strongly positive social attitudes, including those among the young, towards self-employment.

The persistent, if perhaps waning, role of the family in the Italian social system goes far to explain this paradox. Mr. Paolo Garonna, in his address to the Rome conference, pointed out that the family continues to fulfil productive as well as consumption functions in the economy, preserving a tradition of artisan entrepreneurship. In the relative absence of an extensive social safety net, aside from some government subsidies to large enterprises to keep redundant workers on their payrolls, working in the family helps to redistribute unemployment. This setting not only makes the newly unemployed – or those seeking first jobs – relatively more prone to try self-employment than their counterparts in other countries, but also provides a key element of institutional facilitation for the developments in Italian entrepreneurship outlined and discussed in Chapter I (pp. 13-16).

The Italian government spends upwards of two per cent of GNP (1.8 per cent in 1998; see Table 8) on a wide range of programmes dealing with labour market policy. They fall into three main categories, but overlap considerably. First, slightly less than half of the total spending goes to traditional, "passive" income-support policies, but only about a fifth for unemployment benefits themselves. Second, about 39 per cent go into various schemes for economic restructuring and incentives for hiring new or unemployed workers. "Active" policies – creating new firms, supporting self-employment and retraining – come third. Overall policy limits spending on them to ten per cent of the total (8.9 per cent in 1998); the key youth-entrepreneurship initiatives fall under this heading. While one would perhaps go too far in saying that the numerous programmes under these three main headings are fully co-ordinated, they do nevertheless often relate closely and support one another.

Many programmes in all three categories, and especially the more "active" ones in the second and third, are planned and administered at the local and, particularly, the regional level. They thus meet, get co-ordinated with and either complement or are complemented by the numerous local and regional schemes characteristic of the Italian system. The well known territorial pacts (*Patti territorial*) and area contracts (*Contratti d'area*), which concentrate in the South but have spread throughout the country, are part of this system. Both often include specific elements to promote self-employment in general, although they do not necessarily focus on potential young entrepreneurs. Many regional public institutions and credit consortia (*Finanziarie regionale*) also operate, such as E*rvet* in Emilia-Romagna, *Friulia* in Friuli Venezia Giulia and *Veneto Sviluppo* in the Veneto region. They provide start-up support either directly or through guarantee programmes for industrial associations, which offer loans at subsidised interest rates to their members.

Table 8. **Italian Government financial support for programmes related to labour market policies, 1998**

	Amounts			Percentages	
	Lire (billions)	US$ (millions)	Euros (millions)	Of total	Of GNP
Passive policies (income support)	17 993	8 936	9 293	49.0	0.9
Of which: Unemployment benefits	7 741	3 844	3 998	21.1	0.4
Policies for industrial consolidation and employment incentives	14 281	7 092	7 326	38.9	0.7
Active policies for self-employment and retraining	3 280	1 629	1 694	8.9	0.2
Training in regional programmes	2 800	1 391	1 446	7.6	..
Youth entrepreneurship (l. 44)	300	149	155	0.8	..
Self-employment incentives	180	089	093	0.5	..
Administrative costs	1 200	596	619	3.2	..
Total	36 754	18 253	18 892	100.0	1.8

Note: Based on government expenditures in GNP accounts.
Source: Belussi (1999), Table 9.

In this institutional nexus, the funds effectively available in one form or another, directly or indirectly, to aid enterprise creation surely exceed the amounts of government funding shown directly under the two most relevant programme categories of Table 8. European Union (EU) funds play an important role in many programmes as well. Italian policies for developing new enterprises, conceived as elements of competition policy rather than social policy, have eschewed targeting particular groups of firms or social groups, aiming instead at lowering entry barriers generally. They focus on using credit and credit guarantees (insurance) to overcome the key barrier, capital availability. In the process, the institutional structure has heavily influenced the development of small and medium-sized enterprises (SMEs) and the forms of self-employment. Small firms in Italy's Northeast compete fiercely, for example, and rates of technology adoption have accelerated. Altogether, the competition-policy orientation, the regional and local focus of delivery institutions and the emphasis on practical start-up assistance, complemented by tutorial help, have combined effectively to reach a substantial part of Italy's high population of potential entrepreneurs.

The Italian system for promoting entrepreneurship and self-employment began to develop its present focus in the mid 1980s, with the passage of two pieces of important legislation. Both concentrated initially on the South, the *Mezzogiorno*, where previous large-scale industrial development projects had failed conspicuously and at great cost. Both took a decidedly more "micro" approach, and both have now spread to most if not all of the rest of the country. The Marcora Law (L. 49, 1985) focussed on promoting co-operatives among workers from shutdown plants. Co-operatives are important in the Italian economy. In 1998 they numbered over 3 800, with more than 118 000 members (Belussi, 1999, Table 12, p. 3). The even more famous De Vito Law (L. 44, 1986, amended by L. 275, 1991, and further bolstered by L. 236, 1993) aimed directly at assistance to young, new entrepreneurs. Both laws pioneered the strategic linkage of self-employment promotion with active policies to combat unemployment. Law 44 has special interest for this book because it focuses specifically on self-employment among the young.

The institution spawned by L. 44, *Imprenditorialità Giovanile* (IG) S.p.A., has become a widely respected model of "best practice". It began as a national committee based in Rome, then in 1994 became a corporation. The Italian Treasury owns 84 per cent of its capital, with minority positions held by the country's principal co-operative federations. Mr. Carlo Borgomeo, a former trade-union leader has led the organisation from the start. Capitalised at 12 billion lira (US$6 million, €6.2 million) IG had 234 employees and a turnover of 63 billion lira (US$31.3 million, €32.5 million) in 1998. Its original mandate was to support new-firm formation by young entrepreneurs, aged 18 to 35, in the South. Its tools to do so included 1) non-reimbursable financial subsidies of up to 60 per cent of capital costs; 2) loans for an additional 30 per cent of capital costs; 3) three-year loans for administrative and management outlays; and 4) tutoring and training programmes to improve management skills. Thus, IG operates both to deliver financial support from the Italian Treasury and as a service provider. As its success and renown have spread, demand for its services to implement projects to promote entrepreneurship, job creation and local development has expanded beyond the original client, the national government, to regional entities and the European Union.

In its first twelve years of life (through 1998), IG reviewed some 5 700 business plans and approved 1 600, which entailed investments of about 3 900 billion lira (US$1.937 billion, €2.014 billion). These projects

© OECD 2001

created about 26 000 new jobs, mainly in manufacturing.[19] In fact, IG can take a significant share of the credit for the new export dynamism of southern Italy. Of some 990 firms that received financing, 800 had begun operations by 1998, with about 13 000 employees, annual turnover of over 1 600 billion lira (US$795 million, €826 million) and an 80 per cent survival rate after five years. Once their public subsidies ended, their survival rates more or less paralleled the 50 per cent for firms in the economy as a whole. As beneficiary firms became economically viable, they returned the value of IG's investment in them to taxpayers in seven years, on average. To achieve these results, IG received allocations of public funds totalling 4 777 billion lira (US$2.372 billion, €2.467 billion), about 75 per cent of which were invested directly; the rest went for training and administrative costs. IG also administers programmes partly funded by the EU; they totalled 1 096 billion lira (US$544 million, €566 million) in 1998.

With the legislative changes in the early 1990s, IG expanded its operations to other regions. By the end of 1996, 29 per cent of its project approvals and financing, as well as 34 per cent of the resultant new job creation, had taken place in Italy's Centre and North (Belussi, 1999, Table 10, p. 30). In that year, IG received another substantial expansion of its mandate – to promote and finance self-employment among all age groups nation-wide, in Southern Italy as well as some 900 municipalities in the Centre and North. The vehicles include extensive training and a subsidised loan programme (no grants), under which approved projects can receive up to 50 million lira (roughly 25 000 US dollars or euros) for capital costs, plus a fifth of that for overheads. The financing programme was allocated 180 billion lira (about 90 million US dollars or euros) in 1998 alone. The criteria for financing include the quality of business plans and their probability of success. In only the first two years of this programme, IG evaluated 49 000 business proposals, of which 27 500 were eligible for financing and 2 300 became actual start-ups, involving 105 billion lira (US$52 million, €54 million) in total investment. It admitted 17 000 eligible applicants to entrepreneurial training courses and started 300 such courses, with 5 600 participants.

In Italy, Law 44 – and IG S.p.A. – enjoy a wide reputation for success, for many reasons:

- Italy's South was a difficult place to start, a daunting proving ground, with a history of expensive, failed "macro" industrialisation policies.

Yet IG succeeded in creating enterprises, youthful entrepreneurs and thousands of jobs, in manufacturing rather than only commerce or services, and at much lower costs. It helped to restore "positive" entrepreneurship, weaning society away from dependence on the state and public-sector employment, in areas otherwise dominated by poverty and "destructive" entrepreneurship, namely crime.

- IG has built for Italy a professional capability in evaluating business plans and training new entrepreneurs. It also has enabled innovative forms of local partnerships among public, private, non-profit and voluntary institutions.

- Both the underlying legislation and IG have demonstrated the feasibility of active, "micro" policies for job creation, entrepreneurship and local development. They have shown that such programmes can have financial sustainability and can go where markets often fail to reach in initial capital funding, investment banking for small projects and entrepreneurship training.

- Despite high levels of subsidy, highly discretionary intervention and centralised decision making, neither the law nor IG's operations have distorted competition or displaced jobs. Where they have operated, especially in Southern Italy, no competing activities existed to be displaced. Moreover, dead-weight effects have been small because most of the new entrepreneurial activities and the new jobs they generated would simply not have come to life without IG's help.

IG S.p.A. remains the most important institution with a specific focus on young entrepreneurs and co-ordinated programmes for training and start-up help among its mandates. Many others, not necessarily oriented towards younger entrepreneurs, round out the picture. Aside from the previously mentioned regional public and private entities, FORMAPER, for example, began its life as a regional organisation created by the Milan Chamber of Commerce, specifically as a trainer for entrepreneurship and self-employment. It has become both well known and active in selling its services internationally, with about 100 employees specialised in entrepreneurship training. Its core activities provide such training courses in schools and universities throughout Milan and Lombardy, seminars for new and established entrepreneurs and artisans, and practical information. It does research on self-employment for regional and national governments, the European Commission and private firms. SPI (*Promozione e Sviluppo Imprenditoriale*)

© OECD 2001

S.p.A., owned indirectly by the Institute for Industrial Reconstruction (IRI), had already become a leading Italian institution for promoting entrepreneurship and job creation by the mid 1980s, with a central focus on business incubation. New legislation in 1989 and 1993, dealing with problems in areas touched by steel-plant closures and aimed at creating at least 7 300 jobs, provided SPI with a total of 800 billion lira (US$397 million, €413 million) in funding.

The Italians have also thought about ways to transmit enterprises – going concerns – to young entrepreneurs. A partnership between a networking organisation, the Committee for Young Entrepreneurs, and the National Confederation for Crafts, has set up a database project on enterprise transmission. It will gather information on entrepreneurs interested in transmitting their knowledge and ultimately their businesses to younger owners, and, initially, evaluate these firms' values, profits, market shares and technology. It has three objectives:

- To ensure the survival of firms that risk disappearance when their proprietors reach advanced age, even when they employ competent people and have important market shares, know-how and competitive technology.
- To preserve the employment associated with these firms.
- To provide younger entrepreneurs with concrete possibilities in such businesses, with tutoring by elder entrepreneurs to reinforce their professional and entrepreneurial skills.

France[20]

Mr. Phillippe Salles, Director of one of France's most important youth entrepreneurship programmes, DEF*i jeunes* (Youth Challenge), summed up his presentation at the Rome conference with the following statement. *"France has reached a crossroads. The resources are more than sufficient, the public will is manifest and the new programme, 'Services (for) Youth Employment' (nouveaux services/ emplois jeunes) has contributed to a better understanding of the interrelations between the classical economy and an economic society united in the service of local development. It now remains definitively to make enterprise creation commonplace, as a natural path alongside initial training, continued education and job alternatives to bring young people into the professional workforce."* This statement highlights a contradiction that many French observers believe impedes the emergence of a vibrant entrepreneurial economy in France, especially among the young: despite amply financed and relatively well organised (but not always well co-ordinated) programmes, enterprise creation remains less popular than they believe ought to be the case.

The official manifestation of political will became even more evident in early April 2000, with the announcement by Prime Minister Jospin of a wide range of new measures to promote enterprise creation[21]. He called encouragement of "the spirit of enterprise" one of the priorities of the Government, and the Finance Minister, Mr. Laurent Fabius, termed enterprise creation "a great national cause". The new measures (see Box 1) represent essentially a reinforcement of existing mechanisms for active promotion of entrepreneurship, along with a forceful declaration of policy and a real effort to eliminate residual governmental impediments to enterprise formation.[22] These initiatives are not limited to younger entrepreneurs, but the government clearly had youth in mind in drafting them.

The most important sea change in French policy on youth entrepreneurship actually occurred in the 1997 legislation that established the *nouveaux services/emplois jeunes* programme. This law essentially formalised the French approach in a more "active" labour-policy framework. The current new initiatives carry it forward. Along with a 1998 law concerned with "the struggle against exclusion", it made creation of their own activities by the young a "right", which, *inter alia*, gave them access to a panoply of practical support, including enterprise financing, relief from employers' social contributions and follow-up help and counselling. Just as important, it also stimulated and supported both numerous public programmes at all levels of government and many private initiatives to invest in all aspects of support for youth entrepreneurship.

It is necessary to put the role of the French State in perspective. Salles (1999) speaks of the profusion and great diversity of often competing groups that support youth entrepreneurship. A recent count recorded some 1 830 of them, public and private, although they are often too compartmentalised, lack synergy and thus do not adequately replicate "best practice". Nevertheless, they function within a distinct schematic architecture.

Although the central government is a major source of funds, it plays an operational role essentially of observation, analysis and facilitation. The Paris ministries funnel funding largely through regional and local governments,

Box 1. **Highlights of new measures to promote enterprise creation in France, announced by the government in April 2000**

Finance

Loans for small, local projects. Individuals can receive loans up to FF50 000 (US$7 300, €7 600) tied to new business formation. Neither interest rates nor other conditions have yet been fixed, but the programme envisions up to 30 000 loans, or total funding of FF1.5 billion (US$220 million, €230 million). Local governments will be invited to participate in the programme, which associates the state, the BDPME (Office of Small and Medium Enterprises) and the CDC (*Caisse des Dépôts et Consignations*).

Risk capital. A risk-capital fund, of FF1 billion (US$146 million, €152 million) will be put together by the state, the CDC and the European Investment Bank (EIB), alongside another created in 1998. The new fund is chiefly for sectors with long-term promise, such as biotechnology. Another, existing public source of funds for seed capital and business incubation will receive FF100 million more (about 15 million US dollars or Euros).

EDEN extended. With FF400 million (US$59 million, €61 million), this mechanism to encourage new enterprise development (*encouragement d'entreprises nouvelles*) will see its life extended to the end of 2002. It offers reimbursable advances as part of the programme for aid to the unemployed who create enterprises (*l'aide aux chômeurs créateurs d'entreprise*, or Accre).

Fiscal and social measures

Business angels. These are private, outside investors in young small and medium-sized enterprises. Under the 1998 budget law, they received a deferral of profits on investments in firms younger than 15 years old, but only once. The current proposal would allow the deferral as often as the capital is reinvested in new companies. A bigger population of Business Angels will be encouraged by a reduction to three years from five in the time that an investor must keep funds in a company, and a drop to 5 per cent from 10 per cent in the minimum share of the company's capital that the investor must hold.

Repeal of business-formation taxes. The 2000 budget law had already done away with business-registration taxes. The new measures would do the same for several small, special stamp and other taxes. The state will now collect nothing from the formalities of business establishment.

Mobilising collective Savings. The tax regimes covering risk-capital societies (SCR) and investment clubs will be simplified and/or made more flexible.

Social charges. Without giving details, Prime Minister Jospin has announced that reductions in employers' social contributions from which young business owners already benefit will be increased.

Unemployment insurance. Currently, an employee who leaves a job to found a business loses all rights to unemployment compensation. The Government will look at ways to ameliorate this lack of coverage, as part of a renegotiation of the system now underway.

© OECD 2001

> Box 1. **Highlights of new measures to promote enterprise creation in France, announced by the government in April 2000** (*cont.*)
>
> **Incorporation**
>
> *Capital requirements.* From now on, the minimum capital for a limited-liability company (SARL) of FF50 000 can be paid in over five years, thus reducing the effective initial capital costs to FF10 000 (about 1 500 US dollars or euros).
>
> *Capitalising know-how.* If the partners of a new business agree, it will now become possible to capitalise the knowledge and skills (*savoir-faire*) of an entrepreneur, up to a limit of FF50 000.
>
> **Administrative simplifications**
>
> *Internet portal.* By the end of 2000, the government will have established an internet portal to all the sites that could interest a potential new entrepreneur, providing a sort of "one-stop shop" for all the documentation and procedural steps involved in founding a new business.
>
> *Commission for further administrative improvements.* The Government has charged a joint group of entrepreneurs and relevant government officials to propose further administrative simplifications within a few months, for all aspects of enterprise creation.

which have strictly circumscribed economic-policy functions but nevertheless form the principal channels for service delivery and for involving private business groups and associations. The Regional Councils have heavily exploited their responsibilities for regional planning and development (*aménagement du territoire*) to create tools for the establishment, co-operation with and financing of enterprises. Some have encouraged and built innovative voluntary organisations. Nord-Pas de Calais, for example, has joined a number of public and private partners to form a solidarity fund (*Caisse Solidaire*) to finance small enterprises. In Poitou-Charentes, the regional planning school (*l'École régionale du projet*) has a large range of measures to help business formation, including training, tutorial help, financing and business incubation. The Auvergne region has a scheme to give young graduates with viable projects a year's financial aid to devote full time, with mentors, to pursue them. More broadly, and particularly in the communes (city and even village governments), understanding of the local benefits of supporting young entrepreneurs has spread widely. In a good example of this, 30 medium-sized French cities formed in 1998 a network of communes to stimulate business formation.

Salles (1999) stresses, however, that support networks for young founders of businesses depend heavily on initiatives of private groups and associations. They often specialise in specific sectors. Some closely guide their clients. Others concentrate on various forms of financing (seed money, loans, guarantee funds or provision of risk capital). They take various organisational forms permitted under French law, which offers a relatively rich panoply of choices for voluntary and quasi-public associations. Foundations created by large private businesses play a particularly strong role.

DEFi *jeunes*, created in 1987 and funded by the Ministry of Youth and Sports, has operated since 1990 as a *Groupement d'Intérêt Public* (Association in the Public Interest). One of the main French programmes, it provides a full range of services to support both enterprise formation and innovative projects of all types among people aged from 15 to 28 years. It reaches its clientele through a network of about 100 "correspondents", who receive clients, orient them and evaluate their projects. As the projects begin to form, it intervenes by mobilising networks of people with expertise in particular types of projects, providing candidates with financing to obtain expert advice, project evaluation, counselling and training. At the project-formation stage, it offers interest-free loans that can reach FF50 000 (US$7 300, €7 600) for clients over 18 and a fifth of that for younger ones. In addition to its own, official resources, it successfully mobilises strong participation from other public and private sources. In its first twelve years of life, DEFi *jeunes* raised FF160 million (US$23.5 million, €24.4 million) in such sponsorship, which more than matched its own outlays of FF140 million (US$20.5 million, €21.3 million). Finally, when the projects are under way, it follows up with further counselling and training, as well as help for the young entrepreneurs (its "laureates") to form and maintain contacts among themselves and with others.

A recent study of all the young people helped by DEFi *jeunes* since its origin reveals considerable information about how active programmes of this type touch and impact upon their client populations in socially positive ways. The programme has reached people at all education levels; half were post-secondary students and half had a secondary education (the French BAC) or less. A third were unemployed and seeking work, and these were by far the most creative. The programme's training and counselling activities had lasting effects; although many clients did not form their own businesses right away, some 35 per cent of them did so some years later. Whether or not they actually became entrepreneurs, clients reported strong improvement in their psychosocial aptitudes, including the discovery of new capabilities, greater self-confidence and better integration with their economic and social environments. This often involved closer identification with their communities; they found small but viable niches, offered new services and developed new forms of work and work organisation. They also spread intra-generational demonstration effects, as they hired other young people and shared their experience with other young entrepreneurs just starting.

The *Fondation Trois Suisses*, headquartered in Paris, exemplifies a fully private activity, but is a rather special one. Unlike most other private groups in France[23] and other countries, it confines its help exclusively to logistic start-up assistance. It chooses its clients in a panel process to evaluate project proposals. The winners receive a "quality label" and, more tangibly, access to premises and tools such as telephone, fax and Internet, as well as a network of advisors, mentors and potential clients. The Foundation provides neither finance nor training, but the advisory/mentoring process is close and sympathetic. Clients can use its facilities without charge for six to ten months as their businesses get started, then return thereafter for meeting rooms or exhibition space. The Foundation has a current capacity to accommodate about 70 fresh prizewinners every quarter.

Three other examples will illustrate how the many regional programmes operate. The first, ATAC (*Aide Technique, Aide à la Création*), works with the local committee for project assistance. Set up in 1991 to target 18-35 year olds, it provides counselling, financial grants and, over three years, help in accounting and management. Some 95 per cent of the participants are unemployed or have minimal incomes; they come with projects of all types, including business start-ups. With a budget of FF150 000 (US$22 000, €23 000), the programme can finance about ten projects a year after administrative expenses. The second, *Entreprendre et Innover* ("Set Out and Innovate") works in Poitou-Charentes. It holds project competitions for potential entrepreneurs of all ages, with supplementary prizes for winners under 26 years old. Managed by the Regional Mission for Enterprise Creation every quarter, the competitions provide winners with FF100 000 (US$14 700, €15 200) plus a year's use of financial management tools as a first prize, FF50 000 as a second prize and FF25 000 as a third prize. Winners under 26 receive an additional FF25 000, plus a separate, privately funded prize of FF10 000. Between its inception in 1989 and the end of 1995, this programme distributed a total of FF4.9 million (US$720 000, €747 000) in prizes to 60 winners, whose businesses directly created 300 new jobs.

The third example, much larger than the other two, involves the 3CI programme, which began in Marseilles and has grown in fifteen years into operations throughout the Bouches-du-Rhone region, in Lyon and in the *Région parisienne*. Its target population is a challenging one, namely youth in the most disadvantaged parts of the cities in which it operates. Most of its clients are unemployed and/or receive social-assistance income, with no money and very often no skills to found their own businesses. The programme collaborates closely with France's *Association pour le développement et l'insertion économique* (A*die*), in financial partnerships with the CDC, the F*onds d'action social* and the F*ondation de France*, and with local governments. It offers a full range of services: reception; tailored training, mentoring and counsel; follow-up after clients form their micro-enterprises; and capital subsidies of FF30 000-FF40 000 (roughly 4 500-6 000 US dollars or euros). The 3CI initiative has helped bring 4 500 small businesses to life, including 458 in 1999 alone, when 2 600 young clients passed through its doors.

To sum up so far, France has a plethora of relatively well funded programmes aimed at start-up assistance and associated training for young entrepreneurs. Although the State functions as a major source of funds, it plays a largely facilitative role in actual operations, with service delivery focussed regionally and locally through both governments and private groups.[24] The regional, local and private programmes, often small but effective, usually bring their own funding as well, and many of them involve close co-operation among these groups in individual programmes. co-operation and co-ordination among the many programmes is less developed, however, and many synergies and the easy transmission of "best practice" may be lost. The regional and local focus helps to reach a significant portion of the potentially entrepreneurial youth population. The policy approach is distinctively "micro" in its delivery techniques and thus well adapted to the problems posed by youth unemployment in modern, post-industrial economies. While the French themselves still look upon their society as insufficiently entrepreneurial, they have in fact made great strides, perhaps because of that perception. On the basis of youth-entrepreneurship programmes in place, and their accomplishments, France stands as a leader rather than a laggard in this field.

© OECD 2001

What about entrepreneurship education? The analysis so far has looked at various types of training tied to schemes for start-up assistance, but it has not focussed on pedagogical activities not linked to such help, whether curricular or extra-curricular. In France – as contrasted with Italy, for example – one begins to see a relatively large number of such initiatives at all levels of schooling. They may not yet be as well developed or extensive as in some other countries, but innovation is taking hold. As pointed out in Chapter I, French critics argue polemically for a veritable revolution in French education, away from excessive valuation of traditional diplomas and towards a system which stresses technical competence, flexibility, initiative and entrepreneurial habits of mind. Although perhaps more evolutionary than revolutionary, such changes have begun.[25]

Building Awareness. Both public and private initiatives in schools seek to raise awareness of business ownership and self-employment as a viable career option. Two national public schemes deserve mention. Both involve partnerships between the Ministries of Education and Labour, with strong participation by others at the local level. Neither of them stresses business creation as necessarily a goal, but both aim rather to raise awareness about how firms operate. *Entreprises Cadettes* works with the co-operation of local businesses and banks; it targets pre-baccalaureate students that have chosen specialisation in science and technology. Some 17 000 have participated since the programme's inception. The participants draw up business plans with the help of mentors, then work with computer simulations of start-ups that require them to take decisions typical of everyday life in a small firm. Academic and national juries evaluate the projects, to provide some recognition for good performance. The *Graines d'Entrepreneurs* ("Seeds of Entrepreneurship") programme, implemented through a partnership with regional governments and local chambers of commerce and industry, targets junior high-school students. It too offers entrepreneurial simulations. For nine months (the school year), participants work with a methodology but no formal technical support; they receive an address book of professionals available for counselling if they want it.

There also are regional programmes. *Jeune Entreprise* (Young Enterprise), for example, involves co-operation between banks and the governments of the Loire, Bretagne, Auvergne and Paris regions. It reaches high-school students, who work with business people and teachers over a full school year to establish fictive firms, sell shares and learn what is involved in producing a marketable product or service. A similar, single-region programme, *Apprendre À Entreprendre* ("Learn to Be an Entrepreneur"), operates in Poitou-Charentes. It begins each autumn, with university training for *lycée* teachers and administrators, to give them a sense for enterprise culture and the necessary intellectual tools to guide their students. In the second phase for the rest of the school year, the students, with the help of their professors and support from a business owner, an accountant and a banker, set up and run a fictive firm in each school. The best projects are selected and recognised in a regional competition. Finally, an example of a private programme comes from the *Fondation Trois Suisses*, which, separately from its main operations described above, organises events throughout the country to educate and acculturate young people, informing them about business start-ups and encouraging both their creativity and their knowledge of current affairs.

Higher-Level Business Education. More formalised education in entrepreneurial business skills also has begun to come to French universities. Although these efforts remain scattered and not yet the norm, they are at least available to students that wish to seek them out. The University of Bordeaux has a post-graduate programme in business start-up and project management, for regular students, people aspiring to work in start-up assistance organisations[26] and managers who want to set up their own businesses. At Paris-Dauphine,[27] undergraduates can take pluridisciplinary training in business start-up and development leading to an Entrepreneurship Certificate.

Among French business schools, the Entrepreneurial Centre of the *Ecole Supérieure de Commerce* ("Sup de Co") at Lyon offers both a programme in start-ups for young entrepreneurs and a specialisation in "Enterprise Creation and Entrepreneurship", which attracts about a third of the school's students. The "Sup de Co" at Pau offers a similar specialisation. HEC, one of the top business schools, has a programme to give final-year students hands-on experience in starting up, consulting, sales and communication. The ESSCA in Angers has a three-part programme in start-up, take-over and transmission of firms; its students get contacts with business incubators, bankers and start-up assistance programmes, as well as six-month internships.

Professional schools other than business schools, especially in engineering, also make business education increasingly available. The *Institut*

National des Sciences Appliquées in Lyon offers its final-year students a module on start-ups, using case studies and hands-on experience. The Ecole des Mines in Alès provides 90 hours of teaching on start-ups, including a business-simulation exercise, to second-year students, and it has a business incubator for graduates with technological projects.

Although not strictly a part of the educational system, Junior Enterprises (JEs) form a network of student associations that actually do business and learn much by doing so. The associations are always linked to educational institutions and function in parallel with them. They operate both as supplementary, extracurricular educational tools and as professional entities, providing students with practical marketing, start-up, management and other business skills. This idea, hatched in France in 1969, now is Europe-wide. The European confederation of JEs, the Junior Association for Development in Europe (JADE), represents 12 countries and co-ordinates ten others, managing a total of about 300 Junior Enterprises. Formed in 1992, it has had support from the European Commission since 1996.

The JEs themselves are self-financed and non-profit. They sell consulting services (chiefly market and sectoral studies) to all sorts of businesses and institutions, public and private. Because they are non-profit and organised under a special legal form for student associations with economic goals, they have fiscal and other advantages, which make their costs low and their services highly competitive in the consulting market. The JE "seal", or charter, can be obtained by any association in an accredited graduate school (offering four or five years of study beyond the BAC) that meets status, educational and professional criteria set by JE and adheres to rules set by the JE national committee (CNJE). Operational controls are strict; each JE must work with a chartered accountant, have constant supervision of its tax situation, ensure that its members study ethics and other governance-related topics, and undergo annual assessments and quality audits. France has 114 accredited JEs, with an annual turnover of FF100 million (US$14.7 million, €15.2 million).

The United States[28]

The United States presents a sort of paradox. On the one hand, it has a highly entrepreneurial culture. Some forty per cent of its young people finishing secondary school express high interest in forming their own businesses, and the tertiary educational system is replete with fully developed courses and curricula, some of them mandatory in the business schools, that make entrepreneurial training easily and readily available. Start-ups occur in the United States in enormous numbers. On the other hand, however, government programmes, except occasionally very local ones aimed at disadvantaged youth, give practically no attention to singling out entrepreneurial activity among young Americans for special encouragement. To be sure, rich official resources are available to help new entrepreneurs in general, but they make no distinctions in availability by age group. They do, however, take special care to serve and encourage other groupings within the population that Americans obviously consider more in need of help – minorities, the economically and socially disadvantaged, women, military veterans and the disabled. Special programmes for these groups have a fairly high probability of touching younger people within them, but this occurs much more by serendipity than by design. In addition to the dynamic field of post-secondary entrepreneurial education, therefore, *"The impetus for promoting and supporting youth entrepreneurship in the United States comes from the non-profit and private sectors, not from public policy."* (Dabson and Willson, 1999, p. 6).

What are the official resources available to promote entrepreneurial activity in general in the US economy? Their central repository and delivery mechanism lies in the US Small Business Administration (SBA), which has been in business for many decades within the Department of Commerce. The SBA offers a complete range of services: access to training and counselling, start-up and business expansion help, a large and complete collection of information resources, different kinds of contacts including local ones and, perhaps most important, a series of loan-guarantee programmes that facilitate small-business borrowing of from as little as US$10 000 to as much as US$1 million. SBA guarantees 75 per cent, up to US$750 000. It provides no grants or subsidised loans, but the guaranteed loans from private lenders contain some subsidy element because their interest rates are capped at relatively small premiums over the prime rate.[29] SBA delivers its services through a nation-wide network of local SBA offices, business information centres, and "One-Stop Capital Shops" (OSCS). The OSCS are partnerships between SBA and local communities, in distressed areas and targeted at "under-served" communities, which SBA looks upon as its new markets. The SBA's counselling resources include its nation-wide Service Corps of Retired Executives (SCORE).[30]

The US Department of Labor, spurred by legislation sought by the current Administration and passed during the 1990s, has many major programmes to deal with youth unemployment, although they do not focus on youth entrepreneurship. The 1994 School-to-Work Opportunities Act provides seed money to state and local partnerships to co-ordinate educational reform with workforce and economic development, lifting academic standards and better preparing youth for higher education and careers. In 1999, some 470 000 youth received work experience with 136 000 participating employers, as part of an integrated curriculum. The 1998 Workforce Investment Act recast the federally funded system of job training and employment services around a one-stop delivery system in each locality.[31] Youth receive a broad array of co-ordinated services. One programme, Youth Opportunity Grants, earmarks US$1.25 billion over five years to reduce poverty and unemployment in locales with the greatest needs, among youth aged 14-21. Another provides US$12.5 million in Youth Offender Grants to test innovative ways to combine job training and juvenile justice programmes so that troubled youth can finish school and find jobs. A third is the Job Corps, a residential training and employment programme serving 65 000 disadvantaged youth through 120 centres, which deliver training, work experience, physical rehabilitation and development and counselling.

In an exception to the general rule, one agency has taken a modest lead in promoting entrepreneurship, including youth entrepreneurship, as part of a regional development effort. The Appalachian Regional Commission (ARC), a partnership between the federal government and the governors of 13 Appalachian states, launched in 1998 a three-year, US$15 million effort to build entrepreneurial economies in Appalachia.[32] Programmes include funding for youth-enterprise projects, conferences and scholarships to promote entrepreneurial training and education, and financial support for convening youth-enterprise professionals.

In the private and non-profit sectors where practically all US organisations for youth-entrepreneurship promotion concentrate, a 1998 survey by one of them, the Corporation for Enterprise Development (CFED) identified some 25 national groups and 22 with a state or local focus (Dabson and Willson, 1999). This likely seriously undercounts the programmes themselves, for at least three reasons. First, many of the national organisations have multiple programmes. Second, they deliver them through local mechanisms, which sometimes might be counted separately in other national settings. Third, small, local initiatives may well have been missed, given the large size and dispersion of the US economy. In any event, the national organisations predominate.

Unlike in many, indeed most OECD countries, moreover, few of the US programmes stress start-up assistance, finance or access to it and practical mentoring of young businesses.[33] Instead, most programmes focus largely on youth-enterprise awareness and training. This probably represents a rational response to perceived market demand. For prospective entrepreneurs, entry barriers generally are low or absent, the financial system is both more developed and more accommodative in funding new firms, official resources like those of the SBA are available in relative abundance and the tertiary educational system has integrated entrepreneurial training thoroughly into its curricula. The key impediments to youth entrepreneurship are attitudinal – insufficient knowledge or awareness among potential young business founders of the possibilities and techniques for creating their own enterprises – and social, affecting minority and disadvantaged youth cut off from the acculturation and training more readily available to the rest of the community.

Some organisations focus on teaching in schools the values and basics of creating and running businesses. Some support school-based programmes by developing curricula and training teachers. Others offer experience by giving young people the opportunity to work in small businesses. Most do not regard business start-ups as the most important outcome of their work, but instead stress staying in school and seeking higher education, leaving participants to see self-employment as a viable future option. Most also target secondary-school students particularly, although some work with community colleges[34] and others with elementary and middle schools. Teaching techniques vary widely, along the full spectrum from traditional classroom training to an exclusive focus on hands-on learning. For students at appropriate levels, the business plan is a widely used teaching and evaluation tool. Largely following Dabson and Willson (1999), the descriptions below cover five examples of major national organisations that both typify the population and represent instances of best practice in the United States.

Junior Achievement, hardly a newcomer, has educated young people from elementary school through secondary school about business and economics for 75 years. In the United States, it reaches about two million students annually with programmes taught by volunteers

© OECD 2001

from the business community. Programmes for 5-12 year olds explain basic economic concepts, emphasising the relevance of economic learning to the workplace and the individual. Middle-school courses explore career options and teach the first steps in marketing and exploring international business. Secondary-school programmes focus on economic theory and practical experience in creating mini-ventures. Junior Achievement has 232 operations spread over all 50 of the US states. It also has gone global, operating in more than 100 countries, including several OECD countries where it is often cited as among the key local institutions building entrepreneurship awareness.

The National Foundation for Teaching Entrepreneurship (NFTE) introduces teenagers in low-income, disadvantaged communities to business and entrepreneurship by teaching them how to found and operate their own small businesses. It works in more than 100 schools, with 3 000 students completing its programme each year. NFTE also leads in training teachers of entrepreneurial skills. In a programme at Babson College (itself a pioneer and leader in university-level entrepreneurship education), it offers a four-day course, based on a longer, 108-hour curriculum that trains students to perform all the basic functions of starting a business. The course, which leads to a certification, equips trainers to use the NFTE's programme materials in their local courses.

Educational Designs that Generate Excellence (EDGE) trains teachers almost exclusively, offering its services primarily to other non-profit organisations. Since its creation in 1993, it has trained over 3 000 people. It now operates its "Edge University" programmes in over 30 US cities, the Caribbean islands, Puerto Rico and Canada. Its classes deliver about 50 hours of entrepreneurship education over three intensive days, preparing students to design their own in-school courses and after-school programmes and to set up business camps. Teachers learn how to start real student businesses and customise their offerings to the needs of their own students. As with the NFTE courses, the EDGE training focuses on using pre-packaged EDGE materials, essentially turnkey course materials in EDGE's case, in local school settings.

REAL Enterprises, a national network of state organisations, works in partnerships with schools to provide courses, curriculum materials, professional teacher development, funding for student businesses and evaluation. It operates in 33 states and, unlike many other groups, covers a full range of educational and other institutions – 140 elementary and middle schools, 250 high schools, 69 community and technical colleges, four universities and 18 community-based organisations outside the educational system. Unusually as well, it also stresses entrepreneurial training in both rural and urban settings. Although REAL is oriented towards training rather than start-up assistance, many of the student businesses that begin as part of the training, especially among young adults, survive and generate employment.

The Marion Kauffman Foundation has a remarkably wide range of activities, managed through its American Institute for Entrepreneurship Education, Institute for Teaching Entrepreneurship Education and Center for Entrepreneurial Leadership. Multiple awareness and training programmes, operated both inside and outside the traditional educational system and often using experiential techniques, cover all age groups. Among them are YESS!/Mini-Society, for children aged from eight to twelve years, and EntrePrep, a programme for high school seniors, which includes a seven-day residential course, workshops and internships in entrepreneurial firms. The Center for Educational Leadership's Clearinghouse on Entrepreneurship Education (CELCEE) provides a valuable information and research function. In partnership with the Center for the Study of Community Colleges, CELCEE also is an adjunct of the US Education Resources Information Center (ERIC) system, a federally funded network of clearinghouses in various educational subfields.

Post-secondary entrepreneurship education in the United States, now solidly ensconced in the academic establishment, has become a ubiquitous, billion-dollar enterprise. Courses and full curricula are taught in more than 1 400 schools – in the business schools, certainly, but also in undergraduate and non-business graduate schools. Elements of the field can be found in practically every academic discipline. One estimate suggests that in the business schools alone some 250 000 to 300 000 students each year take courses in entrepreneurship or small business. The academic and business infrastructure supporting the entire enterprise has become the world's largest source of textbooks, Websites, simulations, trade books, dedicated academic journals and published research on entrepreneurship. The trend feeds back into other parts of the US educational system; nearly a dozen universities now are involved in entrepreneurship training in primary and secondary schools. It also feeds outward, internationally, as universities and business schools abroad (notably in OECD countries) dip into the waters. Almost every US entrepreneurship academic of associate professor rank or higher has active involvement with one, often several, schools or programmes outside the United States.[35]

A fairly safe conclusion, therefore, would hold that, for any US person who makes his or her way through the educational system to an undergraduate degree or higher, a lack of knowledge about entrepreneurship can no longer have much force as an entry barrier to new-business formation. A person, if so inclined, must make some effort to *avoid* entrepreneurship awareness or training. A corollary to this conclusion – indeed, a positive effect of the spread of this kind of education – is that those who decide against entrepreneurial careers will do so on the basis of better, more realistic knowledge and experience than were available to their predecessors.

The United Kingdom[36]

The United Kingdom does not really have a national policy or a governmental apparatus to promote youth entrepreneurship. Although the schools and universities have fairly well developed educational programmes, the task is borne largely by a few healthy, innovative non-governmental institutions. Effective as they are, however, it is doubtful that they reach a majority of the young people that could benefit – and produce the economic benefits – from more awareness, training and start-up help. A more intensive, more well co-ordinated private, non-profit and local effort, or a stronger policy thrust (not necessarily subsidies) from the centre, or both, could tap what appears to be a considerable latent potential for youth entrepreneurship. Scotland, by contrast, shows evidence of more policy co-ordination in this area, even though, as in the United States, youth are not formally singled out for special treatment.

Irwin (1999), reporting on his own organisation's (Project North East's) management of Li*ve*Wire (both are discussed below), indicates that in 1999, among the young entrepreneurs who were the regional finalists for Li*ve*Wire awards, 77 per cent financed their businesses in part from their own funds, 62 per cent from The Prince's Trust–Business (PTB), 47 per cent from banks and 33 per cent from friends and relatives.

© OECD 2001

These figures provide some indication that the banking system plays a major part in financing youth businesses and should not be seen as a major entry barrier. More important, PTB has an even more pervasive role than the banks, assuming that the LiveWire figures are reasonably representative of youth businesses in general.

PTB is an all-round promoter of youth-business start-ups. It provides counsel, training, help with the crafting of business plans, significant funding (grants and loans), mentoring during start-up and accompanying advisory support for up to three years afterwards. The combination of all of these features in a single programme is relatively rare. PTB targets persons 18-35 years old, who are unemployed or underemployed, have few resources, face difficulties in finding other financing, and have good entrepreneurial ideas. For its own funding, it relies on donations (almost 60%), grants from the UK Employment Department and European Regional Development funds (20%) and its own investment income (21%). In 1996, the Employment Department decided to match all private donations, pound for pound, for three years. Its partial support of PBT appears to be the only significant financial display of UK government interest in youth entrepreneurship.

The Trust administers its programme through eleven regions in England, Wales and Northern Ireland and 37 local areas within the regions. A separate charity, the *Prince's Scottish Youth Business Trust*, operates in Scotland. Aside from a few staff managers, the backbone of operations consists of 600 board members and 6 000 advisors, all of whom are business volunteers with specialist knowledge of their communities. Each successful applicant for start-up help is assigned one of the Business Advisors as a permanent mentor. Public, private and non-profit institutions (*e.g.*, universities and local authorities) manage the programme locally.

Between 1983 and 1999, PTB assisted more than 34 000 businesses with almost £25 million (US$39.6 million, €40.8 million) in grants and £56 million (US$88.6 million, €91.4 million) in loans. The top ten of these firms have a total annual turnover of nearly £80 million (US$126.6 million, €130.6 million) and employ over 500 people. Individual loans can go up to £5 000 (US$7 900, €8 200), but the national average is £2 000 (US$3 200, €3 300). Grants are capped at £1 500 (about 2 400 US dollars or euros) and go only to the most needy applicants. Panels of local business people select the candidates, using as principal criteria the applicants' personalities and experience and the business ideas themselves. After selection, candidates get help in preparing their business plans, and their needs for financing, training and mentoring are evaluated and tailored as a package.

Project North East (PNE), an independent, non-profit local enterprise and economic development agency, began its life in 1980. It pioneered in the creative use of the media to accomplish tasks that organisations in many countries try to accomplish through curricular or extra-curricular programmes in education systems. Its evolution also demonstrates how an organisation of this type can build itself through experience. In 1982, it began to run a business competition aimed at young people through a local, commercial television station. The show elicited a heavy response and revealed a market. This led PNE to launch its Youth Enterprise Centres, which offered "one-stop" combinations of counselling, training, access to finance, workspace and common services. On discovering that a foundation it approached for funding preferred to finance clients directly, it began the first of the soft-loan funds that it manages. By 1999 it had raised almost £700 000 (US$1.11 million, €1.14 million), from which it lent over time 2.4 times that amount to youth businesses, in some 500 loans that levered £5.4 million (US$8.5 million, €8.8 million) from other sources.

In 1984, PNE became the regional co-ordinator for *Live*Wire, which Shell UK had started in Scotland two years earlier and since has expanded to Australia, the Netherlands, Chile, Hungary, Oman, Ireland and South Africa, with plans under way for others. In 1986, after a competitive tender, PNE became *Live*Wire's national manager in the United Kingdom. *Live*Wire provides its services to 16-30 year olds. Shell UK provides its main funding, but contributions come as well from local authorities and other private firms. Its annual budget of US$700 000 (€722 000) includes start-up help for new businesses through an awards competition. *Live*Wire's clients begin with an enquiry service, which introduces them to the idea of starting a business and shows them how to find and develop a business idea, to get help and to prepare a business plan. The awards programme follows. In 1998, *Live*Wire handled nearly 23 000 enquiries and received almost 1 000 business plans for the local, regional and national awards competition. The average business turnover of regional finalists in 1999 was £74 000 (US$117 000, €121 000) and average profit on those sales figures was 15 per cent. Average employment was about four people per firm.

According to its own data, LiveWire has passed through a veritable sea change in the nature of British youth entrepreneurship. In 1988, 40 per cent of the start-ups involved people coming from unemployment; only 29 per cent had quit their jobs to found businesses. By 1998, this situation had more than reversed. Some 58 per cent of the regional finalists in the awards competition had left jobs to start firms. The unemployed accounted for only 22 per cent of the start-ups and 26 per cent of those making enquiries.

Among other groups, oriented primarily to more or less classic forms of awareness building and training, Shell UK has another programme, the *Shell Technology Enterprise Programme* (STEP), which each year helps about 1 000 undergraduates in their junior year to secure 8-12 week internships with small businesses. Young Enterprise, a national charity and the UK operation of Junior Achievement, runs three programmes with 2 000 teachers from 1 700 participant schools and colleges and 6 000 volunteer advisors. They reach more than 33 000 students and start up some 2 500 student-run businesses each year. The Company Programme helps students aged 14 to 19, working in teams, to set up and run their own small businesses. The Team Enterprise Programme targets students 15-19 years old with disabilities and learning difficulties. Project Business, a partnership between education and business, gives 14-15 year olds a nine-week programme of business economics, management, etc., presented by a business partner and supported by a teacher.

The system of entrepreneurial education in UK schools and universities is quite well developed. In general, it aims less directly at start-ups than at developing enterprising individuals, no matter what their ultimate career choices may be. There are exceptions, however. Durham University plays a role in the United Kingdom similar to that of Babson College in the United States, as a pioneer and leader in the spread of entrepreneurial education. The Graduate Into Enterprise unit at its Business School, for example, tries to channel graduates into small and medium-sized enterprises (SMEs), and to link that sector to higher education as part of a local development strategy. It has developed a set of teaching programmes to raise awareness, including placement programmes *via* organisations like STEP. It also offers to graduates of any discipline, in its Graduate Associate Programme, a year's training involving employment in an SME and leading to a diploma in Entrepreneurial Management.

© OECD 2001

In Scotland, one gets the impression of a fair degree of coherence and co-ordination in entrepreneurship planning and programmes, driven by a policy called the Scottish business birth-rate strategy and wide recognition that education must change to meet the demands of the modern workplace. Scottish thinking emphasises "enterprise for all", even if younger people turn out to be the main beneficiaries of the programmes. "Enterprise" in this context also means more than just business creation; entrepreneurship is seen as essential for higher employability as well as business formation.

In 1992, a survey to explore why new-business formation in Scotland was woefully below that in England discovered that attitudes were the chief culprit. Neither entrepreneurs nor entrepreneurship had a very high reputation in Scottish society. *Scottish Enterprise*, the main government development agency, became alarmed and decided that three areas needed urgent action: a wide-ranging campaign to change attitudes; a better environment for start-ups; and more entrepreneurship teaching in the education system.

Scottish Enterprise attacked the attitudinal problem with a heavily funded campaign of television, press and radio advertising, a blown-up version of the successful approach which PNE had taken in its region in England a decade before. It and travelling Personal Enterprise Shows attracted considerable attention; some 40 000 people, including many young persons, registered an interest. The campaign now also has a virtual show and self-assessment programme on its Website, at *www.personal-enterprise.org*.

Scotland has had a strong small-business support structure for two decades, so creating a more encouraging environment for business start-ups had to do something more than improve an already good business-support structure. Scottish Enterprise equipped Scotland's 30 *Enterprise Trusts* with training materials, mentor programmes and finance to help business formation further. The Trusts have also been linked more closely with the Prince's Scottish Youth Business Trust and *Live*Wire, and all of them get support from the Scottish Enterprise network of *Local Enterprise Companies*.

Every school in Scotland willing to send at least one teacher for a free, single-day, in-service training course received packs of curriculum support materials, also at no cost, to boost entrepreneurial awareness teaching. There were four packs – three aimed at different student age groups (5-7, 8-12 and 12-14 years) and one for primary head teachers. The penetration rate has been best in the primary schools; secondary schools still present resistance and are now the subject of a new, much more comprehensive Industry and Education Awareness programme aimed primarily at teachers. *Young Enterprise* and a similar industry-led programme, *Achievers International*, are well developed and active in Scottish secondary schools.

In post-secondary education, more than half of Scotland's 43 further-education colleges now include enterprise education as a key element in their curricular strategies; this sector has shown much innovative activity. Moreover, seven universities have taken part in a *University Enterprise Programme* that offers a full-credit course module in entrepreneurship, based on a Babson College model. Some 2 000 students took this module in 1998.[37]

Canada[38]

Canada has an articulated national policy for promoting entrepreneurship, and government agencies are among the leaders in gathering data and conducting valuable policy research on the subject. In the past decade, the national and provincial governments have given much attention to systematic entrepreneurial education in primary and secondary schools.[39] They and the private sector offer a wide variety of programmes for training and start-up assistance. The schemes vary considerably in the age groups that they target[40] and in methods of delivery, but the locus of delivery centres most often on local community agencies and private groups, which ensures that services are tailored to the conditions and requirements of local economies.

The most intensive available programme is a national one, the *Self-Employment Assistance Program* (SEA) offered by Human Resources Canada, a Canadian Government department. It covers all age groups but is limited to previously employed people eligible for national unemployment benefits.[41] This leaves out young people without previous, formal employment experience. According to a 1996 study, most participants are aged 25-44. Only 1.7 per cent are as young as 15-24, although some 17 per cent of all recipients of unemployment insurance fall into this younger grouping (Grant and Dupuy, 1999). This suggests that the benefits reach roughly ten per cent of the eligible population of younger people, with a potential for touching a much higher proportion; the programme faces a known lack of public awareness among potential young participants. Moreover, on a definition of "younger" extended to ages 30 or 35 (as in some countries and some other Canadian programmes), the measured youth coverage of SEA would doubtless be much higher, notwithstanding that the eligibility rules exclude many teenagers and students without insured work experience. The market gap opened by this restriction may explain why several other official and private programmes cater explicitly to students, among others.

The SEA provides a year of training assistance and wage-related insurance benefits but no direct access to capital. Other national programmes have more specific targets or objectives. The *Student Business Loans Program* helps students seeking to operate summer businesses. The *Aboriginal Youth Business Initiative* focuses on this specific ethnic group. The Government funds several other initiatives through its regional economic development and diversification programmes, such as the *Seed Capital and Counselling Program* of the Atlantic Canada Opportunities Agency and the *Western Youth Entrepreneurs Program* of Western Economic Diversification Canada.

The Canadian provinces supplement the national programmes, the SEA in particular, by offering both training and capital, often through guaranteed bank lending. Examples include the *Self-Start Program* in New Brunswick, *Service d'Aide aux Jeunes Entrepreneurs* (SAJE) in Quebec and the *Young Entrepreneurs Program* in Ontario. Many of these schemes also provide counselling, mentoring and consulting services, and many include the production of business plans as a key component. Loans guaranteed wholly or in part can reach C$15 000 (US$10 600, €10 300), but most are for C$10 000 (US$7 100, €6 900) or less.

A fairly large number of private and non-profit initiatives complement the national and provincial programmes. Among the most important of them, the Canadian operation of *Junior Achievement* is one of the oldest non-profit organisations in the country. The *Canadian Youth Business Foundation* is modelled on PTB in the United Kingdom and its wide range of services and financing. The *Young Entrepreneur Financing Program* has some uniqueness as a bankers' programme. Operated by the Business Development Bank of Canada (BDC) in partnership with the Bank of Montreal and CIBC, it targets 18-34 year olds with commercially viable business ideas in their early start-up phases. After project evaluation, preparation of a business plan and a favourable loan decision, it provides capital of up to C$25 000 (US$17 700, €17 100). The new firms receive 50 hours of management support and access to counselling and mentoring as part of a plan tailored to each business, along with close monitoring of business performance.

The thrust to teach entrepreneurship more systematically in Canadian schools is about ten years old. Following a study carried out in the Atlantic provinces in 1990, provincial and federal authorities developed curricula and materials for both primary and secondary schools. In 1995-96, 50 000 students in grades 8-12 were enrolled in entrepreneurship classes, thousands of teachers received training and annual student entrepreneurship conferences became more common. All grade levels from kindergarten through secondary school saw the curricula and materials introduced in 1996 and 1997, and exposure of every student in every grade level to components of these courses will become complete in Canada in the next few years. The teaching approaches vary around the country. In general, however, primary schools (ages 5-12) provide enterprise classes, junior-high students (ages 13-15) get introduced to small business and entrepreneurship in the contexts of other courses, and the high schools (ages 16-18) take a more focused approach on planning and experience in mini-ventures.

In the Atlantic Region, the Seed Capital and Counselling Program mentioned above, offered through the Atlantic Canada Opportunities Agency in partnership with community organisations, has developed specifically complementary programmes for students in each of the main school-age groups and ranging from eight to 23 years old. These schemes allow students to develop business ideas, receive start-up capital and obtain counsel or mentoring. They consist generally of three weeks of business-planning classes with the rest of the school year devoted to setting up and running student businesses. Provincial governments support them with student-venture loans repayable when these experimental ventures conclude – or transform themselves into permanent businesses.

Australia[42]

This subsection must, unfortunately, begin with a programme obituary. Over two years ago, Australia's major youth enterprise promotion programme, the *Youth Business Initiative* (YBI), disbanded after it failed to obtain continued financial support from the Federal Government. White (1999, p. 10) characterises its demise as a distinct *"loss to the services available to young people"*.

YBI's passage from the scene did not leave Australia without significant institutions and resources to promote entrepreneurship among the young, however. While the Federal Government has no schemes that single out potential young business owners, its main self-employment initiative, the *New Enterprise Incentive Scheme* (NEIS), counts about ten per cent of its participants among people aged 18-24. The NEIS is similar to Canada's SEA in its eligibility requirements, perhaps even somewhat more restrictive,[43] and, like the SEA, it provides no loan or grant financing. It does, however, offer a comprehensive and well-focused package of assistance. The package includes training in small-business management, business skills and business-plan development, along with the NEIS income-support allowance for up to a year and mentor advice and support during the first year a business operates. Because a good business plan is one of the products of this package, a client can credibly approach commercial lenders. The training concentrates on providing solid, practical skills in 160 hours of core modules and 40 hours of market research and business-plan development. Its accredited curriculum leads to a Certificate of Small-Business Management.

Two other institutions complement the NEIS locally. The community-based *Business Enterprise Centres* (BECs), many of which are local managing agents for the NEIS, offer wide-ranging support for new or expanding firms, such as advice, training, access to finance, contacts and mentoring. One of the main activities of *Business in the Community Ltd.* (BCL), which is based on a UK model, is support for the BECs. BCL links larger corporations in Australia with local enterprise development.

Australia also has a relatively large number of private and/or non-profit programs. They offer varying mixes of financial help, training (on which financing may or may not be conditional), information and mentoring. The list includes:

- *Live*Wire, adapted from its UK counterpart.
- *Nescafé Big Break*, an awards competition for people aged 16-21.
- *Young Aussie Enterprises* in Tasmania and Victoria.
- Telstra SBDC[44] Young Business Achiever Award, another awards competition.

- *Youth in Business*, a business incubator, which also provides mentor support, finance and training in South Australia.
- *Self Starter*, also in South Australia, providing grants, training and mentoring.
- *South Australian Youth Entrepreneur Scheme*, offering support, mentoring and sometimes loans.
- *Business Ideas Grants*, a private initiative that gives grants as prizes to entrepreneurs of all ages.
- New Enterprise Incentive Scheme, open to all unemployed people.
- *b.generation*, a programme through which the Western Australia SBDC markets a variety of existing business-development services to young people.
- *Australia Self Made Girl*, a business-plan competition for women aged 13 to 21 years, with cash and other prizes, mentor support and work experience.

Entrepreneurship training is available from general business-training organisations (*e.g.*, the SBDCs and the TAFE colleges) which do not cater specifically to younger people. The b.generation programme is in fact one of these, distinctive not because of special services for youth but because of its focused efforts to market its generic services to them. Among the other programmes listed above, Young Aussie Enterprises illustrates an innovative approach not encountered so far in this book. Modelled on a Scottish scheme called *Young Scot*, it uses as its training vehicle what is essentially a youth-oriented franchise operation, the Young Aussie Car Wash businesses in the car parks of large shopping centres. Clients receive training and all the necessary support to set up and run these businesses.

Unlike the other background papers and presentations at the Rome conference, White (1999) identifies gaps in youth-enterprise promotion in Australia – things not done, useful services not offered. The country does not have, for example, any initiatives to build or support either business linkages or networks and associations among young Australian business people. Existing chambers of commerce and the like have little practical utility for them. No programmes exist to promote contacts, exchanges or ventures between young and older business people; the potential for finding systematic ways of passing knowledge and businesses themselves on to young successors as older proprietors retire remains largely untapped. Finally, most programmes concentrate on the birth and the first year of life of youth businesses. Oriented, as White surmises, towards short-term labour-policy goals (*i.e.*, "get youth off the rolls of the unemployed"), they ignore the subsequent opportunities for youth-business development and expansion, where the pay-offs to society as a whole in terms of employment and job creation may become potentially the greatest.

Some other "best practice" examples

The current state of research and knowledge about youth entrepreneurship and its promotion does not permit thorough studies of all the countries in the OECD area. Nevertheless, information is available on some programmes in some countries not already discussed – and some of these programmes are good exemplars, worth pondering by policy makers interested in improving their own schemes.

In **Ireland**, the *Young Entrepreneurs Scheme* (YES) is a public-private partnership operated by Forbairt, the national agency responsible for state support to Irish industry and to counties, businesses and local schools through County Enterprise Boards. Created in 1991, YES targets 12-18 year olds. Its main objectives are to develop a strong enterprise culture in which Irish youth will think about one day setting up their own businesses, help them to deal with a changing employment situation, and encourage initiative, creativity and entrepreneurial skills. Open to all second-level students, YES asks its participants to establish real mini-businesses, sell products or services in or out of school, keep accounts, write business reports and mount exhibitions. In an associated financial-awards competition to judge the business reports, school finalists advance progressively to country, regional and national finals. The programme enlists strong voluntary support from parents and teachers, who form groups to organise the in-school competitions. The Young Entrepreneurs Association, a national committee of parents, professionals and teachers, co-ordinates the overall programme, provides extensive support to local organisers and arranges the regional and national competitions.

In **Greece**, the Ministry of Labour and Social Affairs set up in 1997 an ambitious grants programme to encourage 2 500 new small businesses and self-employed workers. It targets unemployed people 18-25 years old who have technical diplomas.

In **Portugal**, the *Sistema de Apoio aos Jovens Empresarios* (SAJE) provides grants to new businesses, covering 50 per cent of capital needs, plus 10 per cent for projects in distressed regions and another 10 per cent for those aimed at the young unemployed and job seekers. It also provides access to bank capital through guarantees and its agreements with lending institutions. Grants can reach a maximum of 10 million escudos (US$48 000, €50 000). In an innovation not found elsewhere, the grants get augmented in proportion to the number of jobs created by the new enterprise, up to 250. The numbers of new jobs generated, multiplied by 12 times the minimum wage, determine these supplementary job-creation grants – and small multiples of the minimum wage itself (1.5% to 1.7%) are applied if the new employees are unemployed job seekers or women.

The *Wissenschafter Grunden Firmen* programme in **Austria** provides a fairly standard package of finance and tailored assistance, but is targeted unusually narrowly. Operated by the Ministry of Science, it caters to scientists with viable business projects. Most clients are between 25 and 33 years old.

Spain's *Escuelas Taller* programme, started in 1994 and financed mainly by the Spanish National Labour Institute and the European Social Fund, tries to reach the young unemployed (18-25 years old) with limited professional skills. Largely a training programme with income-support benefits, it is built around involving clients in specific restoration and conservation projects as well as those geared towards new services. It provides some 300 hours of tailored job training to about 20 000 individuals in its 700 schools, paying them from 70 per cent to 80 per cent of the minimum wage during the training. Of its three principal schemes, the Enterprise Initiative Centre has most interest here because it specialises in youth entrepreneurship. Students who finish the main training programme receive about 30 per cent of their additional training in basic business fields such as marketing, finance and management, and 40 per cent in case studies, role playing and debate. Those who drop out receive employment assistance. Those who stay and eventually found their own businesses get arrangements for start-up financial support as well as premises and on-site business services.

© OECD 2001

Spain also has an interesting scheme for promoting inter-generational business transfers. Its *Spanish Confederation of Organisations for Entrepreneurs* (CEOE) targets mainly the sons and daughters of entrepreneurs, but also other young people who have finished secondary school and have start-up plans. It encourages the direct transmission of expertise and wealth from parents to children through training and monetary incentives. The programme provides about 1 300 hours of entrepreneurship training over two years and, in a co-operative arrangement with the Institute of Medium and Small Business, a competition in which the best business plans (usually in industry) can win grants of up to Ptas500 000 (US$2 900, €3 000).

International youth-business networks

Like business people of all types, young entrepreneurs in small, new companies have a need to band together in associations that both provide mutual assistance and serve as lobbying bodies nationally and internationally. In the OECD Member countries and the area as a whole, this movement is far less developed than it could be. It has gone farther in Europe than elsewhere.

The *European Confederation of Junior Enterprises* (JADE) has already had brief mention in the discussion of Junior Enterprises in France. JADE tries to develop and spread the international activities of Junior Enterprises throughout Europe, to strengthen recognition of the concept as both a complementary educational tool and a professional endeavour. In international projects, Junior Enterprises often need to subcontract parts of their work to their counterparts in other European countries. Besides facilitating these synergies, JADE helps to create new Junior Enterprises, provides a forum and represents the network *vis-à-vis* European companies and institutions.

Jeunes/UEAPME represents about 180 000 young (under 40) craftspeople and entrepreneurs in the European Union (EU). Founded in 1997, it has seven associations from five Member states. These groups give voice to the needs and interests of their members both nationally and regionally. The network informs its members about European political and legislative developments, represents them before EU institutions and provides a network for business exchanges, transnational projects and youth-business promotion.

© OECD 2001

Yes for Europe, with about 30 000 members, considers itself the main European association of young entrepreneurs, insofar as its membership does not include self-employed craftspeople. Similar to the traditional business organisations, it performs all the typical lobbying functions, tries to improve the economic and social performance of young European entrepreneurs and encourages best-practice activities, particularly in education and training.

The *Young Entrepreneurs Network* is non-European, an American initiative with a presence in over 40 countries. Oriented more towards consulting services and business development, it has the primary goal of building and maintaining an international community of young entrepreneurs. It helps with business resources, exposure and capital access. Its consultants specialise in selling a wide range of specific business services to young entrepreneurs in need of outside help, with initial consultations and project estimates provided free of charge.

The European *Grey Angel* scheme actively encourages the transmission of business expertise from one generation to the next. It is basically a mentoring operation with associated financial and information services. It recruits professionals – early retirees or older people without jobs but with valuable skills and experience – to mentor young entrepreneurs and lead them through start-ups or start-up simulations. After introduction to the programme, selected young firms are allocated Grey Angels to work with them for up to six months, in negotiated and clearly defined roles. The mentors receive allowances and certificate training courses in business mentoring. The firms can also nominate mentors from their own staffs. If a firm does that, it receives a wage subsidy in lieu of a Grey Angel.

Chapter 3

Education, Training and Youth Entrepreneurship: an Analysis

Introduction

Education deserves a separate chapter in this report because it has such a fundamental place in the development of an entrepreneurial society and the economic dynamism that it brings with it. This chapter takes the form of a short essay on policies for entrepreneurial education. It is designed to pull together points and lessons from the descriptive material in Chapter 2. That chapter treated both "education and training" and "promotion" programmes together, because the two cannot really be separated in any practical discussion of policies and programmes to increase the incidence of entrepreneurial ventures in any country. Nevertheless, education is a policy field separate from that of business creation by young people, even if they relate closely. It also presents problems and opportunities that can well be considered independently.

When French commentators and officials insist that the first task of improving the entrepreneurial culture must involve developing a "spirit of enterprise" (*l'esprit d'entreprise*), they have got it exactly right. The concept recognises that, quite aside from teaching specific business skills, even those most useful to young, entrepreneurial businesses, the dynamic effects will not occur unless or until society as a whole accepts and acquires the right habits of mind and behaviour. It also recognises that those habits benefit everyone, not just the entrepreneurs in business for themselves.

It is sobering to realise that formal education, which is a powerful social force in every OECD country, may not always be the route by which entrepreneurial dynamism gets brought to life. Italy, for example, as the previous two chapters have shown, has a very entrepreneurial economy, but its schools do not appear as the primary mover. Instead, other institutions – most notably the family – perform the acculturation function by which people come to view self-employment and founding their own businesses as a viable, even preferred career path, one not to fear but to pursue. Perhaps, because *l'esprit d'entreprise* is so rooted in the Italian culture, which, after all, includes the teachers themselves, formal education almost unconsciously reinforces the general social view, working with it rather than against it. Most countries, however, do indeed look to their education systems as the most appropriate and capable vehicle for fulfilling the acculturation function. Many also currently identify it as the most tenacious obstacle.

The foregoing paragraph implies an important general point. As entrepreneurial education spreads throughout a society, it can create a self-reinforcing mechanism. The "target" is not only just the individual, the pupil or student who may decide to go into independent business or become a successful employee in the modern workplace, but also the whole society with whom the person will come into contact or who will affect his or her life. Family, friends, teachers, social workers, bankers and government officials all exemplify such people. That is why it is a correct approach to begin entrepreneurial education at an early age, without seeing business formation as necessarily its exclusive objective, to make it widely available to all, and to continue it right through university and graduate schooling. This kind of education may well raise the numbers of people, including young people who are the concern of this book, that decide to pursue self-employment, but an equally important effect will be the social reinforcement of those decisions because all will have been similarly educated. Families and friends will support the decisions. Teachers will nurture them. Social workers in disadvantaged communities will encourage them. Bankers will react as positively and as professionally as they can, rather than with a viscerally negative social bias that blinds them to clear analysis of creditworthiness. Government officials will not throw roadblocks in the way, such as taxing new-business creation to the point of discouraging it. Unless or until all of society shares the entrepreneurial spirit, the educational task will not be complete.

Many writers make the point that absolutely no contradiction exists between the educational and training needs of the modern workplace – knowledge and skills, yes, but also creativity, flexibility, adaptability to teamwork and independence of decision making – and those of the entrepreneur, the independent business person. The educational requirements of both successful modern employees and successful entrepreneurs are exactly the same.

This has important policy implications. First, one can have assurance that policies to embed entrepreneurial education in curricula at all levels will equally well serve the larger, recognised needs of educating the workforce and society in general. Second, entrepreneurial education has no "special interest" implications. If anything, it expands the individual's freedom of choice and thus has egalitarian overtones desirable in any democracy, while it avoids the tendency of some traditional educational systems to separate the future "workers" from the future "bosses" too early, reinforcing the class distinctions of the now *passé* industrial era in a socially unhealthy way. Third, because entrepreneurial education can be seen as serving general rather than particular ends, it becomes easier to sell politically. Fourth, to the extent that such education can become generalised, the current veritable hodgepodge of official and private training programmes that try valiantly to compensate for educational failures can eventually be almost abandoned as no longer needed. This will introduce both greater rationality and substantial cost savings to offset, at least in part, the costs of making entrepreneurial education ubiquitous.

In this important field, one need not and probably should not leave everything to the "educators", the education professionals. Beginning with Junior Achievement in the United States 75 years ago and since reinforced by it and many similar programmes in almost all countries, co-operative efforts, especially from the business community, by non-professionals working with the schools have established a viable arrangement for entrepreneurial education, more than a niche. It appears to have gained acceptance almost everywhere, but it needs more co-ordination, more institutionalisation and more resources. There are other players as well, including local authorities and community-based organisations. Their role has grown as economic development emphases have shifted, under the pressures of globalisation, to a local and regional focus. Throughout the OECD area, many successful examples now illustrate how localised development efforts, which unite and co-ordinate the authorities, civic organisations, the business communities and the schools, can boost entrepreneurship, including youth entrepreneurship, as a source of economic dynamism and new jobs. Education to prepare potential entrepreneurs is an important part of that effort. The more localised it is, the more it will retain bright,

© OECD 2001

capable people in the neighbourhood as contributing citizens, effective workers and employers.

Two definitions

Assisting young entrepreneurs requires actions that clearly promote self-employment as a real career alternative for young people. The United Kingdom, the United States, Canada and South Africa, for example, have already introduced new curricula which give to young people information that introduces them to concepts of self-employment. Beyond aiming at stimulating entrepreneurship (*i.e.*, small-business ownership) directly, however, the major objectives of this kind of education are to help develop enterprising people and to teach them self reliance. The OECD (1989) report, *Towards an Enterprising Culture*, stressed more than a decade ago that rapid changes in the OECD economies pointed even then to a need for "being enterprising" that changes in curricula can bring about. The report underlined the importance of the ability to be creative, flexible and responsible, and of a strong problem-solving capacity – qualities by which it characterised "enterprising" – as major qualifications for the young as they enter the labour market and society.

There are in fact two definitions of "enterprising skills", both of which are of interest here. The narrow definition concerns the development of curricula that encourage young people to regard business creation and self-employment as career outcomes, and to prepare them for such endeavours. Such curricula generally enable young people to learn, often through hands-on experience, about business start-up and management. Most of the programmes described in Chapter 2 do precisely that, and many, even if their major focus is on financial and logistic assistance to new youth businesses, find themselves forced to provide such teaching to fill large gaps left open by educational systems.

The broader definition *"regards enterprise as a group of qualities and competencies that enable individuals, organisations, communities, societies and cultures to be flexible, creative and adaptable in the face of, and as contributors to, rapid social and economic change … Its focus is not therefore about learning about entrepreneurism (as in the narrow approach) but about personal development."* (OECD, 1989)

These two definitions lead education theorists to think of "enterprise education" as encompassing the broader one dealing with social skills and attitudes (creativity, self reliance, etc.) and *"entrepreneurship* education" the narrower one, geared more towards the small-business community and venture-related activity. These are useful distinctions, but one must be careful lest they lead to false educational policy conflicts between them. The OECD study suggests that entrepreneurship education is in fact just a subset of enterprise education, concerned with the application of enterprising qualities in the creation of a business venture.

The distinctions are useful in measuring educational outcomes, in two ways. First, programmes such as the National Foundation for Teaching Entrepreneurship in the United States have other goals than start-ups alone. The Foundation seeks to encourage socially positive livelihoods in America's inner cities and to provide young people with an alternative to drugs and crime by revealing productive ways to use their energy. In this kind of programme, the narrow definition does not stand-alone. The social value of personal development is just as important in the outcome.

Second, the social benefits of personal development through learning entrepreneurial business skills, even within programmes whose goal is to increase the numbers of start-ups, diminishes the importance of start-ups in quantitative terms, in favour of the general career outcomes of participants. The Irish YES programme, for example, does not see continuation of a business as a measure of success. Its young participants do set up businesses, but their survival and their profits are not taken into account as measures of success. The programme aims to lay the foundations for these people to return to entrepreneurial activity later in life, but not at the expense of higher education. Many US schemes have the same goals. In the YES programme, deeply involved teachers and parents give more importance to its capacity to build confidence, create teamwork, generate an appreciation of work and inculcate understanding of business, finance and marketing.

Many programmes try to provide entrepreneurship awareness (in its general sense) to all ages and groups, in schools and in universities. In Canada and other countries, successful efforts have begun to affect education systems, resulting in innovative curricula and pedagogy to this end. Most enterprise education at all levels in the United Kingdom does not aim directly for start-ups but tries to develop enterprising individuals. Canadian and US programmes reach for the same broad goal as they focus on an understanding of and the motivation for business ownership, but they also tend more to encourage young people to set up in business; in Canada, more than in the United States, they also facilitate it.

Teaching teachers

Entrepreneurial (or enterprise) education cannot even begin until teachers and administrators within an educational system become convinced of its value and trained in its techniques, some of which are highly non-traditional. The same needs for training apply to those in private and non-profit programmes that have teaching or training components, especially when those programmes operate in the schools or in co-operation with them. In the United States, programmes like EDGE and the National Foundation for Teaching Entrepreneurship form a sort of sub-sector of institutions that operate exclusively or in large part to train the trainers rather than the entrepreneurs themselves. The French *Apprendre à Entreprendre* programme has an element of teacher training as well.

The country sketches in Chapter 2 have shown how governments, in Canada and Scotland, for example, have put heavy resources into teacher training as part of their introduction of new materials and curricula. These efforts also reveal how educators can resist such change, as in the Scottish secondary schools. Because they view themselves as the bearers and transmitters of society's traditions as well as its knowledge – as indeed they are – educators can be among society's most conservative forces. Nevertheless, the story of entrepreneurial education's penetration into the OECD area's school systems is more notable for its successes than its failures.

An overall impression persists that these successes have often been achieved with "quick-fix", briefing-session methods to familiarise teachers as quickly and as briefly as possible with new materials and curricula, so that their introduction in classrooms can occur just as quickly. Sooner or later, such methods will have to be replaced by a longer-term perspective on teacher training, one just as concerned with developing "enterprising teachers" as with turning out "enterprising graduates". This provides the surest way of overcoming deeply ingrained resistance to change and of producing a mass of professionally qualified teachers in the field. It is the task of higher-education institutions with specific programmes for teacher training. In the United States, Canada and the United Kingdom, the spread of entrepreneurial education in the university systems probably has extended this acculturation to many who become teachers in schools, yet it receives very little discussion. Still less, virtually nothing in fact, is known about entrepreneurship education in undergraduate and graduate programmes specifically for teacher training. Programmes aimed at this educational sub-sector have not come to light. This subject could bear considerable further research.

Teaching entrepreneurship in primary, secondary and tertiary institutions

Chapter 2 provided a reasonably comprehensive review of how entrepreneurship and enterprise education take place and are spreading in schools. It remains to highlight how such teaching in fact follows certain patterns, notable because they cut across national and cultural lines and resemble one another quite closely in different countries.

At the primary level, what the discussion above characterised as broad enterprise education holds the spotlight. "Acculturation" is in fact the proper approach for young children. This holds true even for private, business-funded programmes like Junior Achievement, which pioneered co-operative programmes in the schools between teachers and outsiders who come in for presentations and special courses. As children enter their early teenage years, the mix between these broader programmes and more focused entrepreneurial training becomes somewhat more balanced, and the focus continues to change in the same direction in secondary schools. One finds more and more programmes that include "hands-on" experiments with fictive or real student businesses, for example, and programme content increasingly emphasises subjects like finance, management and marketing. Thus, while programmes may still have broad acculturation goals and even, as noted above, measure their success largely in terms of them, their actual content becomes more knowledge-based, specific to business subjects and sophisticated to match the greater absorptive capacity and curiosity of older students.

Not all countries deal equally well with serving young people at that crucial crossover point between finishing secondary school and entering university. It is laudable and proper that programmes should emphasise the progression to higher education and the postponement of real entrepreneurial activity for that reason, especially where they focus on rescuing clients and students in disadvantaged social circumstances from lifelong imprisonment in those circumstances. There are, however, people – and one may hope that the primary and secondary schools will have made them "enterprising" ones – who will not want

© OECD 2001

university education or who will make rational choices to pursue trade or craft careers. These people deserve as clean and clear an opportunity to enter self-employment or found their own small businesses as anyone else. Many studies have shown that successful self-employed people often have little university education. An excessive social bias towards higher education or an absence of programmes to help them found their businesses at this stage would not serve them in an egalitarian way. The continental European countries generally provide better programme assistance for such people than do other countries.[45]

At the university level and in graduate schools, the shift to outright entrepreneurship training becomes much more complete. Here, students are after all young adults who are forming or have formed at least tentative career choices. They both need and demand specific, practical training when those choices involve forming their own businesses. The universities may still retain a certain residual acculturation role, but they must also meet the educational demands of their students. This is not a contradiction: if previous education in a system geared towards forming "enterprising" people has in fact permeated the social fabric up to this point, many more people than in the past will indeed make the career choice for independent entrepreneurship. The goal will have been met, and the universities bear the responsibility for the final educational thrust towards entrepreneurship for their students.

As Katz (1999) makes plain, entrepreneurship education has thoroughly permeated the US university system. Canada and the United Kingdom are not far if at all behind, France is pulling up quickly, and one can find at least some entrepreneurship teaching in universities and business schools throughout Europe. Business schools in the United States have not thrown off their traditional *raison d'être*, to train managers for large corporations and financial houses (which today demand "enterprising people" too), but they have added substantial teaching programmes in entrepreneurship to their curricula. Babson College in the United States and Durham University in the United Kingdom have reputations as pioneers in entrepreneurial education. MIT, with all the offerings of its Sloan School of Management, has a huge impact on entrepreneurial activity. Entrepreneurial education also has spread deeply into other disciplines, such as engineering. In the United States, this trend is in one sense self-replicating. Entrepreneurial teaching programmes are awash in funding, much of which, as Katz (1999) points out, comes from endowments provided by successful entrepreneurs.

© OECD 2001

Training

"Training" here refers to educational activities in entrepreneurship conducted outside formal schooling, most notably by programmes whose principal objective is to help young persons set themselves up in business. Many programmes have this content because they must fill gaps and lacunae left open by inadequate formal education. This wastes or at best misdirects resources that might otherwise go into financing and logistic help for young entrepreneurs. The key point to make here is that full development of formal education along the "enterprise education" lines suggested by OECD (1989), with appropriate "entrepreneurial education" added towards the later years of schooling, would greatly reduce the amount of such training that self-employment assistance programmes, public and private, would have to provide. They would still want to make sure that clients prepare adequate business plans and have a proper kit of business skills, but the resources needed to produce these results on the foundations laid by better education would likely become a fraction of those now necessary.

Chapter 4
Conclusions and Some Policy Suggestions

The principal conclusions

This book began with a discussion of the highly intractable problem of youth unemployment, which affects all OECD Member countries and has principally structural rather than macroeconomic causes. The promotion of entrepreneurial activity among young people can help to solve it, even as pursuit of education and training needs, identical for both entrepreneurs and modern workforces, prepares for productive lives people who do not choose to become entrepreneurs.

As the presentation developed, it became clear that support for youth entrepreneurship can play two other important roles in modern economic societies struggling to deal with the changes incident to globalisation. First, new business formation in general and that by young people in particular plays a dynamic role in job-creating growth. Moreover, it meshes with economies' burgeoning needs for flexibility, quick adaptability and innovation to remain competitive in the globalised environment. These attributes of competitiveness flourish in a dynamic, constantly changing small-business sector.

Second, the pressures of globalisation cause economic development strategies to become ever more local and regional. Italy and France exemplify this phenomenon well. In such an environment, success comes when the authorities, the educational establishment, the business and financial communities and community-based organisations band together in co-ordinated development strategies. The promotion of local entrepreneurship, especially among the young, has a central place in such strategies because it accelerates development, localises it and arrests the out-migration of talented people to the industrial centres that characterised the now nearly bygone industrial age. Modern communications and transport make possible the linkage of local nodes of economic activity with the global economy, because they simply wipe away the economic disadvantages of distance and separation.

Following Belussi (1999), more detailed conclusions emerge as well. Many empirical studies, applicable to Italy and other countries, suggest that the self-employed fall into four main groups:

- *Traditional* entrepreneurs, who base their work on professional or artistic competence. This group includes modern manifestations of the old medieval artisan workshop, as well as lawyers, doctors, dentists, independent consultants and the like.
- *Industrial* entrepreneurship, sometimes organised in industrial sub-contracting networks but also including small firms that exploit technological niches or serve increasingly differentiated markets for "boutique" consumer goods.
- *Service* enterprises that have permanence. Note that some of these (fast-food establishments and delivery services, for example) have gained notoriety as unstable career employers, although they can have as much durability for their owners as many other small businesses. (If not, they are the *marginal* entrepreneurs characterised below.) Their insecurity for employees is another matter, but if, as often occurs, they become the locus of first after-school and summer jobs for the very young, they do provide an introduction to the world and disciplines of work. Their most deleterious effects arise when they become career "traps" for the disadvantaged, who can find no other jobs. Many youth-entrepreneurship promotion programmes work specifically to prevent such outcomes.
- Marginal entrepreneurs, often in underdeveloped areas, include those in the informal industrial sector and some new service activities, those who extract cost advantages from black markets, those who exploit themselves and those who briefly provide temporary services.

Countering a view that sees self-employment as "a bitter medicine to cure unemployment", Belussi (1999) proposes another interpretation – that its growth represents *"a radical disruption of the old Fordist regime of regulation, opening up a wide range of possibilities for self empowerment and the 'entrepreneurialisation' of work, moving towards a post-Fordist world of knowledge-intensive jobs."* (p. 18.) The development of such entrepreneurial activity does not have a necessarily positive or negative impact. A complex process, its outcome depends on a number of factors that are either non-economic or only tangentially economic:

- National institutional contexts: access to the health-care system and other social protections for the self-employed, the structure of national pension systems.
- Seemingly contradictory forces, such as a push for more autonomy and freedom, on the one hand, or processes like downsizing, decentralisation and out-sourcing, on the other.
- Whether societies have put in place systems of universal rights, much different from issues of collective bargaining, which promote less hierarchical production systems with extensive co-operation, exchanges of knowledge and informational networks. Such rights include:
    - Access to global communications nets.
    - Strong intellectual-property protections.
    - Continuous education and training.
    - Flexible labour market institutions that facilitate easy entry to and exit from both self-employment and wage work, with portable social protections such as unemployment benefits.

Some policy suggestions

Not all governments have articulated policies that favour and boost youth entrepreneurship. They should have them, given the positive impacts that it can have on youth unemployment, economic growth, job creation, local and regional development and economic dynamism.

The notion of "articulated policy" has several aspects. Perhaps most important, it may or may not but does not necessarily need to become a full-blown, resource-intensive, programmatic, subsidised approach. Some governments will prefer such an approach and others will not; a debate on the issue here would be a sterile one. The important factor concerns a clear expression of political will and a desire to see a co-operative effort to promote youth entrepreneurship in society. From that can flow many facilitative, low-cost things that governments can do to foster much-needed co-operation and co-ordination among competing programmes, such as organising conferences to push the players to recognise natural synergies among themselves, providing centralised information banks and both supporting and disseminating policy-oriented research. These services are needed in any case, even if governments decide on more ambitious policy programmes – which many do, with measurable success.

Youth entrepreneurship has a constituency, in the large parts of populations that are under, say, 30 years old and the networks of national, private, community and local-government institutions that promote it. The rapporteur at the Rome Conference has suggested that youth entrepreneurship may indeed be more than an employment strategy for young people and in fact an educational and social strategy to prepare the future workforce for the demands placed upon it. If "dressing it in enterprise clothing" helps to sell it and gain political support, so much the better. It is clear that the entire movement, as it has emerged and is described in this book, combines policy responsibilities that cut across ministerial lines in all governments. At the very least, those concerned with the new, flexible labour market policies and with educational policy will need to take it into account and co-ordinate their approaches.

If it is reasonable to expect that state-funded youth-entrepreneurship programmes will, with some notable exceptions, be fairly modest and emphasise encouragement rather than financial support, then more of the burden will shift – or continue to shift – to private and non-profit organisations, with implementation more likely local than national. This leads to some policy suggestions for these organisations as well:

- **The field must become more institutionalised**. Too many programmes in too many countries operate in a species of competition rather than co-operation. More co-operation need not necessarily constrain the laudably entrepreneurial nature of the best-practice programmes in the field, but it would better husband scarce resources, build public credibility and perhaps generate more funding support. To start, programmes could form and participate in national and international networking institutions or associations, hold conferences to exchange best-practice information and formulate agreed criteria for effective practice.

- **More programme evaluation is needed**. Government-run programmes usually do measure results because public accountability and interministerial competition for scarce budget funds demand it, but non-government programmes are deficient in this respect. In the absence of hard rather than anecdotal evidence of success, programmes risk discrediting the claims of practitioners and supporters, not to mention sub-optimal or even deficient voluntary funding.

- **Establish more co-operative connections with others.** Notwithstanding many examples of programmes working with educators, social and youth services, community organisations and local economic development programmes, wide opportunities exist for intensifying such co-operation. While presenters often go into the schools to introduce entrepreneurship topics or run entrepreneurship programmes, how many of them work closely with teachers to find ways concretely to link academic achievement with entrepreneurship? How many programmes working in disadvantaged neighbourhoods have effective ways of co-operating with social assistance groups, public and private, to deal with non-entrepreneurial issues like drugs, crime, child abuse, health and nutrition? Are working relations with public and private community-development organisations close enough and sufficiently productive?

- **Young entrepreneurs need more networks and support groups among themselves.** Aside from a scattered few groups that have formed, mostly in Europe, youth entrepreneurship promoters pay little or no attention to helping young entrepreneurs to band together in information-exchange networks, to provide mutual help to one other and, perhaps most important because they are indeed a constituency, to represent and lobby for them. This gap in service probably arises because those who promote youth entrepreneurship operate too much in competition and too little in co-operation.

Notes

1. Excerpt from a speech at a congress on youth entrepreneurship, Imagin'Enterprise, Paris, Palais des Congrès, 29 November 1999. The French text reads: "Si la création d'entreprise est une aventure personnelle et individuelle, c'est aussi l'affaire de la société tout entière. Car ses bénéfices sont collectifs. La création d'entreprise est en effet la clé de la croissance et de l'emploi. C'est d'elle que dépendent, à moyen terme, la prospérité et le rang de notre écomomie sur la scène mondiale."
2. Much of this chapter draws heavily on a background paper prepared for the Conference: Blanchflower and Oswald (1999).
3. The declining proportion of youth in the labour force may have arisen from a declining youth population or, more importantly, a drop in the youth participation rate. The source (Grant and Dupuy, 1999) stresses the latter.
4. Atlantic Canada comprises Newfoundland, Prince Edward Island, New Brunswick and Nova Scotia. The prairie provinces are Manitoba, Saskatchewan and Alberta.
5. Data from Statistics Canada, 1996 *Census*.
6. Female high-school dropouts are far less likely than male dropouts to participate in the labour force, however, and those who do so experience an unemployment rate about twice that of male dropouts. Teen pregnancy likely is an important contributing factor.
7. These are three of the 17 statistical categories used by the Australian Bureau of Statistics (ABS).
8. The ABS (1997) Characteristics of Small Business Survey, Canberra, found that 66 per cent of small business operators and 78 per cent of those ABS defines as microbusinesses (fewer than five employees) worked from home.
9. These data exclude Germany.
10. But not salaried employees who work at home under one of the newer industrial practices of this electronic age.
11. Official and public resistance to educational reform in some countries, and not only that of the established intelligentsia, may well reflect fears of the breakdown or rearrangement of class distinctions, to the extent that educational systems reinforce them.
12. This section draws heavily on Blanchflower and Oswald (1999).
13. OECD (1997), *Labour Force Statistics*, OECD, Paris.
14. Although they come originally from the same source, Tables 2 and 3 are not fully comparable because the years differ, and the percentages in Table 3 measure self-employment relative to the employed labour force in each sector. Table 3 indicates that, for the economy as a whole, self-employment occupied 24.8 per cent of the working labour force in 1996, up from 23.2 per cent in 1980, whereas Table 2 shows the self-employed at

14.7 per cent of the total working-age population in 1994, down from 19.6 per cent in 1970. One would need comparable unemployment data and information on participation rates to ascertain whether they partly or wholly explain these differences.
15. All conversions of local-currency figures into dollars and euros in this book are based on the exchange rates prevailing on 3 March 2000, with the conversions usually rounded to the nearest 1 000 currency units.
16. Eurobarometer (1990). See Blanchflower and Oswald (1999), Tables 4 and 5.
17. See Blanchflower and Oswald (1998); Evans and Jovaanovich (1989); Holtz-Eakin, Joulfaian and Rosen (1994); Black, De Meza and Jeffreys (1996); and Lindh and Ohlsson (1994), p. 1515-26.
18. This subsection draws heavily on Belussi (1999), pp. 14-18 and information provided by the Italian youth entrepreneurship agency IG S.p.A.
19. Under L. 44, IG initially favoured goods-producing enterprises in agriculture, industry, small business and handicrafts. Law 236 expanded this range to include cultural assets, tourism, civil and industrial maintenance, environmental protection, technical innovation and farming.
20. This subsection draws heavily on Salles (1999).
21. Reported in *Les Echos*, 12 April 2000.
22. In the past, France was not reluctant to tax business formation. Now, the Prime Minister has said, "The State soon will not touch a single franc from the creation of an enterprise." (*Les Echos*, 12 April 2000, p. 2)
23. The *Françoise Douce Association*, for example, specialises in giving prize money to young entrepreneurs (under 30) for start-ups in the media and communications. In an annual contest, it selects the 15 most innovative projects submitted, offering prizes ranging from FF 10 000 to FF 100 000 (1 500-15 000 US dollars or euros).
24. Non-French observers may find this system difficult to comprehend in full, especially if they live in systems, as in Germany or the United States, where concern for the separation of powers between central, state and local governments has a long tradition. In France, more than these others, power and authority tend to flow more hierarchically from the central to the local level, with more concern for the division and delegation of powers than for their separation. While this can sometimes lead to excessive bureaucracy, it can, at its best, be highly efficient.
25. The critics rightly argue that attitudinal change among employers and educators is key. Signs appear increasingly that such change is taking hold. Regular readers of France's business newspaper, Les Echos, will see good evidence of this, in regularly appearing articles and opinion pieces describing reorientation of training programmes for the unemployed and shifts in the "quality" aspects of labour demand. Human-Resources directors in French companies, for example, frequently cite their de-emphasis of formal qualifications in hiring policies and greater stress on the skills, adaptability and teamwork orientation required in modern labour forces. See, for instance, the issues of 29 May 2000, p. 4, and some points made in a two-part series on unemployment, 30-31 May 2000, pp. 78-79 in each issue.
26. Note how this is becoming a profession in itself, a sure sign of institutionalisation.
27. One of the schools in the University of Paris system.
28. The basic sources for this subsection are Dabson and Willson (1999) and Katz (1999).

Notes

29. The prime rate is the rate at which banks lend to their largest and best customers. Most firms do not receive it and pay considerably more. The SBA's US Government guarantee of 75 per cent of the loans both overcomes banks' hesitations about credit risk and significantly lowers the interest costs of small-business borrowing.
30. Complete information on the SBA and its operations (including, for example, details like terms and interest rates for the several loan-guarantee programmes), organised and tailored for easy use by prospective entrepreneurs, can be found on SBA's widely praised Website, www.sba.gov. Navigating the site is easy, notwithstanding its size. The site map alone is five pages long, and the substantive pages run cumulatively into the hundreds. A related site maintained by SBA's Office of Advocacy (for small business), www.sba.gov/advo, contains other information that will interest researchers, including data, analysis and research.
31. The SBA's OSCS are part of this increasingly popular "one-stop" concept, although they do not stem from this legislation. They result from the Administration's 1994 Empowerment Zone (EZ) initiative to revitalise distressed inner cities and rural communities through federal-local, public-private partnerships. SBA makes an OSCS available to each EZ community.
32. This region, geographically more or less coincident with the north-south Appalachian mountain chain a few hundred miles inland from the East Coast, has long remained relatively underdeveloped in US economic terms. In the mid-20th century it was by reputation America's economic mezzogiorno.
33. One of them is the MIT Business Plan Competition, which has led to the establishment of 30 companies that have raised US$43.6 million in capital and created 500 jobs.
34. "Community" or "junior" colleges are more or less unique to the American system. They are post-secondary institutions that draw local students and offer two-year courses of study, which correspond roughly to the first two years of standard college or university instruction, but often with a more professional than general educational orientation.
35. The foregoing observations come from Katz (1997), which provides not only a complete description of the phenomenon but also a history of how and why it developed and grew.
36. This subsection draws on Irwin (1999), with the comments on Scotland based on Burton (1999).
37. Burton (1999) provides further points and details, and a fuller policy context.
38. The principal source for this subsection is Grant and Dupuy (1999).
39. Not much information is available on post-secondary entrepreneurial education in Canada, but there is little reason to doubt that it is fairly well developed, along lines parallel to those observed in the United States.
40. Definitions of "youth" vary from programme to programme in those that are targeted towards youth rather than the general adult population, from a minimum of 15 years old to a maximum of 35.
41. Eligibility also includes participants in the Atlantic Groundfish Strategy (TAGS).
42. This subsection is based on White (1999).
43. Eligible applicants must be over 18 years old and not yet qualified for the Australian Age Pension, unemployed, registered for full-time employment and in receipt of an unemployment allowance or pension. Their proposed businesses must be new, "greenfield" operations, independent (not subsidiaries, franchises or exclusive contractors)

© OECD 2001

and assessed as commercially viable by an NEIS Advisory Committee. They also must not compete directly with existing businesses, unless they fill unsatisfied demand or provide goods or services in a new way. This last requirement – open to wide bureaucratic discretion in both its good and bad senses – appears to differ greatly from policies, as in Italy for example, which focus simply on reducing entry barriers and let competition take its course. The NEIS programme is described in detail in OECD (1995).

44. "SBDC" stands for Small-Business Development Corporation.
45. In addition, Germany and France both have well-developed apprenticeship systems, and the French one is becoming increasingly entrepreneurial. Recall, also, how the Europe-wide Jeunes/UAEPME represents and lobbies for young craftsmen.

Bibliography

ABS (Australian Bureau of Statistics) (1997),
  Characteristics of Small Business Survey, Canberra.

BELUSSI, Fiorenza (1999)
  "A Framework of Analysis of Self-Employment in Italy", LEED document [DT/LEED(99)7], Territorial Development Service, OECD, Paris, April-May.

BLACK, J., De MEZA, D. and JEFFREYS, D. (1996)
  "House Prices, the Supply of Collateral, and the Enterprise Economy", *Economic Journal*, No. 106, January, pp. 60-75.

BLANCHFLOWER, D.G. and OSWALD, A.J. (1998)
  "What Makes an Entrepreneur?", *Journal of Labor Economics*, No. 16, January, pp. 26-30.

BLANCHFLOWER, David and OSWALD, Andrew (1999)
  "Entrepreneurship and the Youth Labour Market Problem", LEED Document [DT/LEED(99)11], Territorial Development Service, OECD, Paris.

BURTON, Tony (1999)
  "Youth Entrepreneurship in Scotland, The Planning Exchange", paper prepared for the Rome Conference, November, available at LEED Programme, Territorial Development Service, OECD, Paris.

CONTINI, B. and PACELLI, L. (1995)
  "A Study on Job Creation and Job Destruction in Europe", mimeo, R&P, Turin.

DABSON, Brian and WILLSON, Jennifer (1999)
  "Youth Entrepreneurship in the United States", Washington, Corporation for Enterprise Development, Paper prepared for the Rome Conference, available at LEED Programme, Territorial Development Service, OECD, Paris.

EUROBAROMETER (1990)
  European Youth, No. 34.2, Fall.

EVANS, D. and JOVAANOVICH, B. (1989)
  "An Estimated Model of Entrepreneurial Choice under Liquidity Constraints", *Journal of Political Economy*, No. 97, pp. 808-927.

GAUTHIER, James and ROY, Richard (1997)
  "Diverging Trends in Self-Employment in Canada", Human Resources Development Canada, Applied Research Branch, Strategic Policy, Document No. R-97-13E, Ottawa.

GRANT, Gerald A. and DUPUY, Damian A. (1999)
  "Youth Employment and Entrepreneurship – An Overview of Canadian Experience and Policy Considerations for the Future", Toronto, CGA Consulting, paper prepared for the Rome Conference, available at LEED Programme, Territorial Development Service, OECD, Paris.

HOLTZ-EAKIN, D., JOULFAIAN, D. and ROSEN, H.S. (1994)
"Entrepreneurial Decisions and Liquidity Constraints", *Rand Journal of Economics*, No. 25, Summer, pp. 334-347.

IRWIN, David (1999)
"The Growth of Youth Entrepreneurship in the UK", Project North East, Newcastle upon Tyne, Paper prepared for the Rome Conference, November, available at LEED Programme, Territorial Development Service, OECD, Paris.

KATZ, Jerome (1999)
"A Brief History of Tertiary Entrepreneurship Education in the United States", paper prepared for the LEED Programme, Territorial Development Service, OECD, Ref. [DT/LEED(99)4], Paris, OECD.

LIN, Zhengxi, PICOT, Garnet and YATES, Janice (1999)
"The Entry and Exit Dynamics of Self-Employment in Canada", Statistics Canada, Analytical Studies Branch, *Research Paper Series* No. 134, Ottawa, March.

LINDH, T. and OHLSSON, H. (1994)
"Self-Employment and Self-Financing", *Economic Journal*, No. 106, November, pp. 1515-26.

NATIONAL CENTER OF EDUCATION STATISTICS (1997),
Digest of Education Statistics, 1997, Chapter 5, Web site: http://nces.ed.gov/pubs/Digest97.

OECD (1989)
Towards an Enterprising Culture, A Challenge for Education and Training, Educational Monograph, OECD/CERI, Paris.

OECD (1995)
"Self-Employment Programmes for the Unemployed", Papers from a joint US Department of Labor/OECD international conference held in Washington in 1995, OECD Document [OECD/GD(95)1040], Paris.

OECD (1997)
Labour force Statistics, OECD, Paris.

OECD (2000)
Employment Outlook, OECD, Paris.

PICOT, G., MANSER, M. and LIN, Z. (1998)
"The Role of Self-Employment in Job Creation in Canada and the United States", paper presented at the Canadian Employment Research Forum (CERF)-LEED International Conference on Self-Employment, Burlington, Ontario, 24-26 September.

RAPITI, F. (1997)
"Lavoro autonomo, lavoro diopendente e mobilità: un quadro statistico", in Bologna, S. and Fumagalli, A. (Eds.): *Il Lavoro Autonomo di Seconda Generazione*, Milan, Feltrinelli.

SALLES, Philippe (1999)
"L'Entreprenariat des Jeunes en France", Paris, DEFi Jeunes, November, paper prepared for the Rome Conference, available at LEED Programme, Territorial Development Service, OECD, Paris.

SERIEYX, Hervé (1998)
"A New European Context for Youth Employment", paper available at LEED Programme, Territorial Development Service, OECD, Paris.

SESTITO, P. (1989)
"Alcune note sull'occuoazione indipendente in Italia", *Economia and Lavoro*, Vol. 13, No. 3.

SPIERINGS, J. (1998)
"Young People, Skills Development and Employment Growth", paper presented to the Australian Local Government Association Regional Economic Development Forum, Canberra, November.

STATISTICS CANADA (1998)
Self-employment and Youth Unemployment, Labour Force Updates, Labour Force Survey, Catalogue No. 71-005-XPB, Ottawa, Statistics Canada.

TACKEY, N.D. and PERRYMAN, S. (1999)
Graduates Mean Business, Brighton, Institute for Employment Studies.

WHITE, Simon (1999)
"Youth Enterprise Promotion in Australia; An Overview with Best-Practice Highlights", paper prepared for the Rome Conference, available at LEED Programme, Territorial Development Service, OECD, Paris.

© OECD 2001

OECD PUBLICATIONS, 2, rue André-Pascal, 75775 PARIS CEDEX 16
PRINTED IN FRANCE
(04 2001 03 1P 1) ISBN 92-64-183795-X – No. 51645 2001